THE

ORVIS®

STREAMSIDE GUIDE TO

TROUT FOODS AND THEIR IMITATIONS

THE ORVIS®

STREAMSIDE GUIDE TO

TROUT FOODS AND THEIR IMITATIONS

Tom Rosenbauer

Illustrations by Rod Walinchus

**Photographs by Tom Rosenbauer,
Henry Ramsay, and Ross Purnell**

Skyhorse Publishing

Skyhorse Publishing books may be purchased in bulk at special discounts for sales promotion, corporate gifts, fund-raising, or educational purposes. Special editions can also be created to specifications. For details, contact the Special Sales Department, Skyhorse Publishing, 307 West 36th Street, 11th Floor, New York, NY 10018 or info@skyhorsepublishing.com.

Skyhorse® and Skyhorse Publishing® are registered trademarks of Skyhorse Publishing, Inc.®, a Delaware corporation.

www.skyhorsepublishing.com

10 9 8 7 6 5 4 3

Library of Congress Cataloging-in-Publication Data is available on file.

ISBN: 978-1-62873-782-0

Printed in China

Contents

Acknowledgments   iv

Introduction   1

1   How Trout Feed   3

2   A Brief Life History of Aquatic Insects   19

3   A Quick Guide to Insect Identification   33

4   How Do You Tell What They're Taking?   43

5   Mayflies   51

6   Caddisflies   78

7   Stoneflies   97

8   Midges   110

9   Other Aquatic Insects   121

10   Terrestrial Insects   133

11   Crustaceans   146

12   Other Trout Foods   155

Index   166

Acknowledgments

IT'S ALWAYS DIFFICULT TO WRITE ACKNOWLedgments for fly-fishing books because you learn something new from nearly everyone you talk to or fish with. For all those I've enjoyed sharing oddball theories with on trout-feeding habits over the years, thanks.

But I would like to offer specific thanks and recognition to people who helped me with the areas I am not as familiar with as I should be. For patient help with my questions, I'd like to thank Thomas Ames Jr., Jim Cannon, Marty Cecil, Jim Lepage, and Craig Matthews. For assistance in providing photographs of creatures I did not have in my own files, thanks to Henry Ramsay and Ross Purnell. And for helping me make sure this book would be truly helpful and my language clear, thanks to my editors Jay Cassell and Nick Lyons.

Introduction

TROUT ARE PREDATORS AND OCCASIONALLY opportunistic. At times, they will eat nearly any small object that falls into the water, sometimes by mistake and sometimes by design. I have seen them eat berries, spiders, houseflies, butterflies, sticks, pebbles, and cigarette butts. But much of the feeding they do is selective, where a rise to the surface or a dart to an unseen morsel below occurs because that object matched a specific "search image" that the trout recognized as familiar and edible.

This selectivity is one of the delights of fly fishing, where we are forced to delude a fish into thinking that a piece of fur, feathers, plastic, and steel is an insect, fish, or leech. For hundreds of years, fly fishers have searched for the perfect fly—the one that will work on every cast. Fly-fishing magazines and catalogs thrive on this conceit.

When I was a teenager, I fished with an older gentleman on a stream known for its difficult brown and brook trout. In a moment of weakness, old Jim told me of a fly he had discovered that would catch trout every time he put it in the water. His face would furrow with concern as he talked about the fly, because he claimed it would ruin fly fishing in our stream if anyone found out about it. He refused to use it ever again in fear that it would destroy his sport. He once gave me a peek at the fly, as he still had some in his box, and with the scruples of your average fourteen-year-old male, I copied a bunch of them at my fly-tying bench.

You know the rest of the story: I couldn't even budge a fish on Jim's fly, but I never told him about it. I didn't want to admit my deceit and spoil his pride. Jim fished on happily for many years, secure in the knowledge that he had the perfect fly in his box, yet principled enough to never use the thing. I think most of us would do the same.

This book is written for the novice and intermediate fly fisher. It's designed to help the person who can't figure out the difference between a mayfly and a caddisfly in flight. It's also for the person who knows his or her insects well, but wants to explore the possibilities of other organisms that trout may eat. This pocket-sized guide won't help you key a mayfly to the species degree. There are many other good books available today if you want to fine-tune your insect identification to that degree. This guide will, however, enable you to identify aquatic insects as members of different taxonomic groups, called orders, such as mayflies, stoneflies, and caddisflies.

All these insects are important as trout foods. Additionally, this guide will help you determine whether other trout foods, such as leeches and crayfish, may be important in your waters. It will also give you a suggested list of imitations you can try if you have no other source for advice—but to be honest, local fly shops and people along the river are better sources for exact patterns to use in your area.

I hope you will keep this book handy in your car, cabin, or kit bag, and that it helps you develop an understanding and appreciation of important trout foods.

1

How Trout Feed

TROUT ARE SHY AND CAREFUL COLD-blooded animals. In contrast to brightly colored blue-gills—fish that feed right under your boat and investigate everything that plops into the water near them—trout are well-camouflaged, fussy about what they eat, and will bolt for cover at the slightest disturbance. Think of bluegills as chickadees and trout as woodcock. A chicka-dee will feed on your windowsill, never try to hide, and can be tame enough to eat out of your hand. Woodcock creep around in heavy brush probing for worms, freeze at the first sign of your presence, and take flight when they think you've spotted them.

Trout evolved over tens of thousands of years to feed in moving water. They are perfectly adapted to preying upon insects. Their streamlined shape allows them to tip up into the current and spear a mayfly nymph from the conveyor belt of moving water that brings them a constant food supply. Their eyesight is sharp enough to spot a tiny midge no bigger than a pinhead when it is still two feet away. Their metabolism is highest when aquatic insects are most active. They can change the color of their bodies to adapt to different stream bottoms; a trout that moves from a dark granite bottom to marble bedrock, for example, will lighten several shades in a few hours. This ability to remain camouflaged allows them to prey on their food supply without being preyed upon in return (except by anglers), which is critical to their survival.

Trout also adapt to still water, revealing their oceanic origins prior to the end of the last Ice Age. In slow pools or lakes, they swim about searching for prey. Although they prefer food that does not run away, when needed they can run down a minnow with blinding speed.

Trout are efficient feeding machines, although they may seem lazy when looked at with an anthropomorphic eye. Over many thousands of years, their tiny brains have evolved into amazing pea-sized computers that can instantly gauge the net energy benefit to be gained from rising through three feet of water to chase a fleeing insect as opposed to plucking a nymph drifting six inches away. Energy used is always balanced metabolically with energy obtained to the point where—perhaps through taste—a trout can instantly judge that eating a mayfly will get them more net calories than chasing a water strider.

DRIFT FEEDING

From the time they are hatched from eggs until they are about fourteen inches long, trout in moving water do nearly all of their feeding by plucking insects and crustaceans from the current. As trout grow, they may become foragers and prowl for bigger food, such as minnows and crayfish. But if insect food is abundant, trout will continue to feed from the drift no matter how large they become. It's an efficient way of getting a lot of food with little expenditure of energy. The current supplies a constant flow of food and all a trout has to do is make sure that what it chooses is worth the effort.

By trial and error, a trout takes up a station on the bottom of a river that lets it stay in place with little effort but is close enough to a flow of water that supplies food. The flow of currents over a riverbed is hardly constant; pockets of slow and fast water are formed by turbulence and the rougher the stream bottom, the more good places there will be for trout to feed. A typical lie would be behind a rock, where a trout can rest in the slow water behind the rock and dart into the faster current on either side. A spot that's nearly as good but not as apparent is the space in front of a rock, where the current piles up and forms a cushion of slow water. Other desirable places are where water rushes over a depression in the stream bottom or where a fast current smashes into slower water and forms what is called a seam.

A trout feeds in the drift by tipping its fins and letting the current push it to a series of spots where it can intersect food. You don't see much movement of the trout's streamlined body because its control surfaces, much like those of a 747 taking off, use the current in such an efficient manner. A trout taking food from the surface lets the water push it up and back slightly. The fish then tips its fins so the current brings it back to the bottom; a small wiggle of its body brings it back to its original position. In the same manner, when a trout sees a piece of underwater food off to either side, it uses the current to push it in that direction.

Dr. Robert Bachman, one of the top trout biologists in the country, received his Ph.D. by spending 5,000 hours in an observation tower studying the feeding behavior of wild brown trout. Because he could recognize each trout by its unique spot pattern, he could determine how much time a trout spent in each position on the bottom of Spruce Creek in Pennsylvania. He noticed that some trout preferred the same position on the creek bottom more than 90 percent of the time and would feed from this one position year after year, not only through the season. Others had three or four preferred spots and would move from one to the other throughout the day. When frightened, each trout had a favorite hiding spot. The shadow of an approaching fisherman or a merganser over the water would send each trout fleeing for a logjam or under a flat rock.

Bachman also observed that trout feeding went on all day when water temperatures were between 55 and 65 degrees Fahrenheit, a range that is optimum for trout. And, unless there was a heavy hatch, trout fed both on underwater nymphs and insects trapped in the surface film without much preference for floating or drifting food.

Bachman also observed that hatchery fish don't always act like wild trout. They seem to lack the ability to gauge the bioenergetics, or potential energy costs versus benefits, of a situation, perhaps because they were bred in concrete tanks with little current. A hatchery trout often darts from one place to another, seldom taking up one feeding position and thus wastes energy. This is one reason hatchery fish rarely survive more than a few months. They literally starve to death, even when surrounded by abundant food.

In slower water, if insect food drifting in the surface film is abundant, a trout will hover just below the surface and feed in a regular manner. This is called sipping. Later on in this book, you'll learn how to identify this feeding behavior.

AMBUSHING

When some trout reach a length of about fourteen inches, they somehow "discover" that more energy can be obtained by ambushing the occasional baitfish or crayfish than bothering with little bugs. This happens more frequently with brown trout than other species. Browns, in particular, become nocturnal or forage heavily when a stream gets dirty after a rain, probably because their prey become disoriented and can be captured with less effort. Radio-implant studies on the Ausable River in Michigan have shown that brown trout will roam more than a mile at night prowling for food.

After dark, large trout that stay hidden under logjams or undercut banks during the day come out and cruise slow, shallow water in search of prey. Small fish that stay in the shallows during the day, partly because they can't handle the heavier current, also tend to stay in the shallows at night. Although this keeps them out of reach of large trout in the daytime, it makes them vulnerable at night when they can't see predators coming until it is too late. Crayfish also come out from under rocks at night to forage the river bottom for carrion and aquatic plants.

Trout can see well in low light and also use their lateral line, which senses vibrations, and their hearing to locate prey.

SELECTIVITY

A trout learns when it is young to distinguish food from litter. The next time fishing is slow, bend down and look into the water. You'll see all kinds of stuff on the surface—cottonwood fluff, sticks, bits of vegetation, perhaps some insects. Unless there is a heavy hatch of insects, most of the surface litter is junk in terms of food value. Somehow, through taste or perhaps texture, a trout learns to distinguish food from garbage. We're not so different, and one reason people become overweight these days is because of the availability of fatty foods. Physically, we're still part prehistoric forager, and something in our chemistry tells us to ingest these calorie-packed bundles because we don't know when we'll get our next meal.

Trout seldom experiment with their diet. They prefer to stick to safe and predictable food. Suppose there is a heavy hatch of a particular species of size 14 cream-colored mayfly every day for two weeks. A hungry trout samples one; its system tells it that the calories obtained are sufficient, so the trout looks for more size 14 cream-colored mayflies. The trout develops a "search image" for the size, shape, color, and behavior of this mayfly. It doesn't perceive a bigger brown caddisfly as threatening or even bad-tasting—it simply ignores the other bugs, just as it ignores sticks and stones drifting past. But occasionally a trout will experiment. If the mayfly hatch is dwindling, the trout is hungry, and that caddisfly makes a twitching movement, the trout now recognizes the caddisfly as something alive and samples it. The trout thus develops a "search image" for the caddisfly at the same time. Fish do seem to have rudimentary memories, so the trout may take a cream mayfly in a few days, even if it hasn't seen one in a while.

Many times there will be a half dozen different kinds of insects on the water. Although a trout might seem to prefer one type over the others, it will be looking for all the insects it recognizes as food at the same time. On the other hand, even though you see a variety of insects on the water, the trout you are fishing for might be seeing only little olive mayflies because the insects drifting over its feeding spot are of only one type. So you try a brown caddisfly imitation and the trout ignores your fly. This is not a casual statement—the trout really does ignore your fly. Unless the fly drags in the current, the trout does not sense any danger associated with your imitation insect. It simply ignores your fly, as it does all the other inedible junk in and on the water.

You will see times when trout don't appear to be selective at all and will take any fly thrown in their direction. This usually happens when there are lots of different bugs on the water, or if you are fishing a stream that does not offer much food and the trout have to take every lifelike tidbit that drifts by in order to survive. Fish in every stream, particularly in these sterile streams, do make mistakes; they sometimes attempt to eat twigs and rocks. As Bachman says, "Every time a trout takes my nymph, he screwed up!"

You can fish only a size 14 Adams for the rest of your life and catch lots of trout. You might do this and concentrate on developing your skills in casting, reading the water, and approaching trout without spooking them. But there will be times when trout will ignore your fly and you will have to be satisfied with a nice day on the water. If you carry a wide variety of fly patterns appropriate to your waters, and if you study the life history and behavior of the foods trout eat, you'll catch more fish—providing your flycasting presentation is lifelike.

HATCHES AND DRIFT

A great hatch, one that brings every trout in the river to the surface, is the event of a lifetime. This kind of hatch does not happen as often as you might think. Most of the time a hatch dribbles insects off the river in twos and threes instead of hundreds. Although there might be a hatch of five insects going on at once, the trout seem to ignore the bugs—at least on the surface. Why are insect hatches so important?

In order to survive, aquatic insects must stay hidden from both predators and the current by living under rocks, in aquatic vegetation, or in the case of caddisflies secured to the bottom in ballasts of sticks and stones. Once a day, however, many of these insects release their hold on the bottom and drift freely in the current. This happens after dark and is a method of recolonizing the lower parts of rivers, because most insects fly upstream to lay their eggs. Trout do feed on these drifting insects, especially early in the morning at the end of the drift, when there is enough light to allow the fish to see the insects. But most of this drift happens overnight when the fish can't see the insects.

Besides nocturnal drift, the other instance when insects are abundant is during a catastrophic drift. This happens when a rise of water increases the current flow and insects get washed loose. Trout feed heavily at the

Aquatic insects stay hidden on the bottom most of the time but are available to trout during periods of drift or when hatching.

beginning of a water rise for this reason. Catastrophic drift can also happen during daily water fluctuations below dams or even when a stream bottom is disturbed by a wading fisherman. In some rivers—notably the San Juan in New Mexico, the upper Yellowstone in Yellowstone Park, and the South Platte in Colorado—big trout will often follow wading fishermen like puppies, feeding on the insects they kick up. The trout get so close that you can't even cast to them, and when you try to shoo them away with your foot they come right back. This has lead to a despicable practice known as shuffling, where the bottom of the river is purposely kicked around to attract trout. This can harm the bottom of the river; moreover, it's unsportsmanlike—don't do it.

THE EFFECTS OF TEMPERATURE

Both trout and 99.9 percent of the foods they eat are cold-blooded, apart from the occasional mouse, lemming, or baby muskrat a giant old trout might sample while feeding opportunistically. The metabolism of the fish has evolved so it is at maximum efficiency when the primary prey is available for capture. During the winter, when water temperatures range from near freezing to 45 degrees Fahrenheit, a trout is mostly inactive. At that time of year, most insects are also buried in mud or inactive under rocks and gravel in the streambed.

In the spring, as water temperatures warm to 50 degrees Fahrenheit, insects begin to hatch and thus are more vulnerable to capture by drift feeding trout. But at 50 degrees, a trout's metabolism is still relatively logy and the fish does not need to eat all day. It is not a coincidence that in early spring, insect hatches occur only during the warmest part of the day. Trout time their feeding accordingly. By May, insects hatch throughout the daylight hours. When water temperatures are in the low 60s, a trout's metabolism is in high gear and perfectly attuned to transforming insect and crustacean flesh into fat, protein, and bone.

If water temperatures rise above 70 degrees Fahrenheit. in the summer, both insect hatches and trout feeding dwindle. A trout's metabolic rate continues to increase, and its body utilizes oxygen at an increasing rate. Now, because warm water cannot hold as much oxygen as cold water can, the trout must become dormant. If the fish did not slow down, its energy demands would outstrip its supply of oxygen so quickly that it would die. In fall, as water temperatures decrease, trout begin to feed heavily again until the water gets too cold in early winter.

The temperature of the water plus photoperiod, or day length, affects the hatching of insects. Each insect species has a particular time of season and temperature when it hatches and mates. Although most of the insects that hatch will be eaten, a small part of the population will survive to meet and mate so the species will survive. Some insect species will hatch for just a few days each season; others may hatch for as long as a month. A few insect species are multibrooded and have two or three hatch periods during the year. Just as you see trillium blossoms only in early spring, wild phlox in late spring, and asters in August, insect hatches are regular and predictable. Knowing the hatching seasons aids greatly in identification.

There are many good books to help you with detailed identification of insect families and species if you choose to go that route. The scope of this book, however, is to enable you to tell a mayfly from a midge and teach you a little of each insect's behavior so you catch more trout and enjoy your time on the water. The chart below is the first of several in this book that will help you pin down what trout might be eating at any given time of year.

MONTHS	FOOD MOST LIKELY TO BE EATEN
December–March	Midge larvae, minnows, stonefly nymphs, leeches, crustaceans such as sowbugs or scuds.
March–April	Mayfly nymphs and adults, stonefly nymphs, minnows, crustaceans, and midge larvae and adults.
May–June (May–August in cooler western and far northern rivers.)	Mostly larger emerging and adult mayflies, caddisflies, and stoneflies. Minnows and crustaceans will also be taken.
July–August	Ants, beetles, grasshoppers, and other terrestrial insects become much more important as aquatic insects dwindle. Mayflies, caddisflies, and stoneflies are mostly tiny—smaller than size 16. Large fish will prowl for crayfish and minnows after dark.
September–November	Both tiny and large mayflies, caddisflies, and stoneflies. Minnows are eaten by large fish on spawning migrations. Midges and crustaceans once again become important, as hatches of aquatic insects become even more sparse.

TYPICAL DAYTIME WATER TEMPERATURE	TROUT FEEDING BEHAVIOR
35°–40°F	Very little movement, which is mostly in bottoms of slow pools. Fish will not chase their prey more than a few inches.
40°–50°F	Trout will become slightly more active at the upper end of this temperature range and may feed on the surface in the middle of the day.
55°–70°F	Trout are active all day long. Fish will chase insect larvae and make splashing rises. Trout will also drift feed below the surface and sip mating insects that have fallen onto the water surface.
55°–75°F	Feeding is concentrated in early morning, late evening, and after dark. Most feeding is more sedate; rises will be more of the quiet sipping variety.
50°–60°F	Feeding is erratic—it can be very active one day and almost dormant the next, depending on weather and geography. Best hatches and fishing are in the middle of the day.

(Continued)

2

A Brief Life History of Aquatic Insects

SOME TROUT FOODS, SUCH AS CRUSTA-ceans and minnows, are active and available to trout all season. But most insects, both aquatic and terrestrial, are dormant during the colder months. Insects are consequently more vulnerable to trout during the warmer months, when hatching from larvae into adults or when returning to the water to lay their eggs. In this chapter, we'll take a closer look at the life cycle of aquatic insects.

LARVAE

Larval aquatic insects are at the wingless stage that live underwater. Most of these live for about eleven months under rocks, in submerged weeds, or buried in the sand and gravel. Trout don't often grub food off the bottom unless it is easy for them to obtain. If cased caddis larvae are abundant, for example, trout might scrape them off rocks on the river bottom—but that is the exception rather than the rule. Larvae are easier for a trout to capture when they are migrating daily in the nocturnal drift or when floods or water fluctuations below dams dislodge them.

Some larvae are also captured and eaten more easily than others. Burrowing mayfly nymphs make tubes in the sand, so a trout doesn't really get a crack at the nymphs until they emerge to hatch into adults. Flat, wide mayfly nymphs cling tightly to the undersides of rocks and seldom venture to the current-washed side of the stones. Other mayfly nymphs swim through aquatic vegetation and sometimes get washed away and eaten. Midge larvae seem to drift more often than other insect larvae, and even though they are tiny, in some trout streams they are so abundant that they are the primary source of trout food. Free-living caddis larvae—the ones that don't build cases—roam the bottom of the river, where they often get carried away by the current.

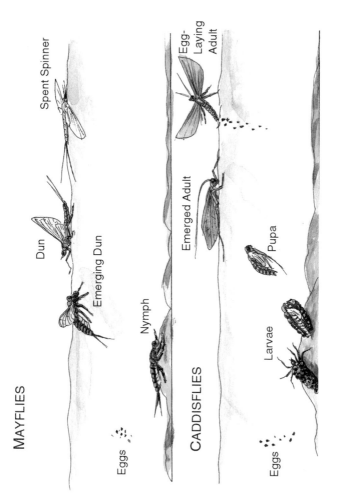

Life cycles of the most important orders of aquatic insects.

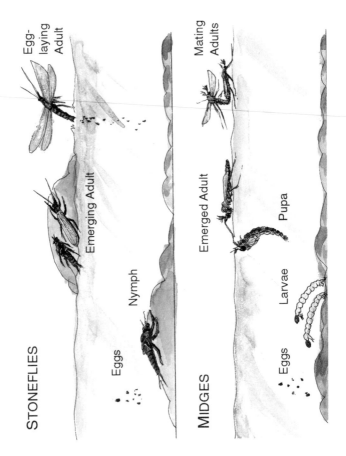

Life cycles of the most important orders of aquatic insects.

(Continued)

EMERGING ADULTS

In many rivers, emerging adult insects are the most important source of trout food. A few days or weeks prior to hatching, aquatic insect larvae get restless and begin to migrate into the shallows in preparation for hatching. For instance, the larva or nymph of the big March Brown mayfly hatches in mid-May on eastern rivers. (The old name "March Brown" comes from a similar-looking English mayfly that does hatch in March.) A week prior to hatching, the shallows are full of these big nymphs, which earlier in the spring lived under flat rocks in the middle of the river. As the nymphs migrate to the shallows, they sometimes lose their grip on the bottom and become part of the drift. Trout learn to recognize them as food, and a big brown imitation nymph will catch trout weeks before you see any hatching adults.

The day a March Brown mayfly hatches, the exo-skeleton of the nymph begins to fill with gases that buoy the insect toward the surface. An insect may drift helplessly in the current for a few feet or, in some cases, for more than a mile before it reaches the surface, splits its skin, and hatches into an adult. Trout are on the lookout for these nymphs and will eat them near the bottom when the nymphs begin to drift and closer to the surface as they hatch. This is a helpless stage for the insect. It can't

A mayfly is most vulnerable when it is emerging from its shuck in the film.

get back to the bottom and most species cannot swim. Trout usually key into the prey they can capture with the least expenditure of energy, and a drifting nymph is perfect.

Mayfly and stonefly nymphs rise to the surface in the same larval stage they were in while underwater. However, caddisflies and midges, like butterflies and other insects that undergo complete metamorphosis, form a pupal stage, which looks unlike either the larva or the adult. This is an important part of the life cycle for imitations. You'll learn more about these insect pupae later when we look at the different insect groups, or orders, more closely.

Once the nymph reaches the surface, it has trouble penetrating the surface tension of the film on the water. The insect will push and wiggle against the surface barrier. At the same time the winged adult tries to wriggle out of its larval skin. (Have you ever seen a movie of a monarch butterfly emerging from its cocoon?) Again, this is an easy meal for a trout, which senses the emerging insect's helplessness. Most fish you see rising at the height of a hatch will be eating emerging insects in the surface film rather than plucking the adults that have emerged and are twitching on the surface, drying their wings.

Why do trout do this? Because the adult winged insects are able to leave the surface of the water abruptly, and an experienced trout soon learns that a winged adult is not a sure meal. A trout that keeps rushing to the surface, only to be rewarded with a mouthful of air, is not going to get much to eat and may not live long. This is why you see small trout leaping for insects while the older survivors sip emerging insects just below the surface. Those youngsters haven't learned to be careful and sedate.

Some insects also crawl out of the water onto rocks to hatch and don't ride the currents as adults unless they get blown into the water. Most stoneflies and craneflies hatch this way, as do a few species of mayflies and caddisflies.

Before the 1970s, most dry flies were imitations of a fully winged adult insect resting on the surface just prior to flying away. This makes sense, because that stage of an insect's life is most visible to us. But our imitations don't

A mating flight of mayfly spinners can be seen by looking into the sun.

always sit on the water as if they were ready to take off. When they slump into the water, they make fine imitations of emerging insects. It seems that we fool ourselves as often as we fool the trout!

There are times when trout will eat fully winged adults on the surface. Most species hatch in riffles at the head of a pool, and in a big river such as New York's Delaware where pools are nearly a mile long, trout in the tail end of a slow pool don't see many emerging insects. Any insects drifting on the surface have usually emerged long before they reach the far end of the pool. Insect wings don't dry well in cold or wet weather, however, so during a rainstorm, species that might ordinarily take flight immediately may drift for many yards before doing so.

EGG-LAYING ADULTS

After an insect hatches and flies away, it heads for a nearby tree or bush to rest. The adult insects are hard to see after they do this, because they rest on the undersides of leaves to avoid being desiccated by the sun. Drying up is as big a threat to their survival as trout or cedar waxwings. Mayflies have a unique life stage, because they are not sexually mature when they hatch as winged adults. The immature winged adult is called a subimago by scientists and a dun by fly fishers. These subimagos molt within a day or two into egg-laying adults, which are called imagos or spinners.

Most other insect species rest during the day and either return to lay their eggs or migrate in early morning or late evening. They copulate in midair or on the water surface. The females then lay their fertilized eggs by dropping them from above the water, dipping their abdomens into the water, or by crawling underwater along the shore. Females and males both eventually fall to the water and die. The entire process of mating, laying eggs, and falling spent to the water takes anywhere from several minutes to several hours. Large mating swarms of aquatic insects can often be seen hovering over the water for hours before they actually hit the surface. This gives you time to plan your attack.

Fishing to spent versions of adult insects is not well understood; some fly fishers even ignore this aspect of fly fishing. However, it often stimulates trout to huge feeding frenzies and produces some of the best dry fly fishing of the season. Timing your dry fly fishing to imitate spent adults includes not only the more famous mayfly spinner falls but also the lesser-known mating flights of midges, caddisflies, and stoneflies.

MATCHING THE HATCH

When fishing for bass or bluegills, the idea is to lure a fish into thinking your fly or lure is just something to eat. Fly fishing for a drift feeding trout requires convincing the fish that your fly is a specific kind of food. The better your fraud, the better your chances of catching a trout. What's most important? Should you fish a gray size 18 caddis imitation if you are sure the fish are taking mayflies but you don't have any mayfly imitations in the right size and color? Most authorities will tell you size is most important, followed by shape, followed by color. An important factor that we often ignore is the attitude and behavior of the fly on or in the water. In fact, I would rank that second in importance, between size and shape.

A Green Drake mayfly dun beside an extended body artificial.

The process of matching the hatch is pretty simple if you have a large selection of flies. It only becomes difficult when you have a slim assortment of flies and need to decide which compromises you should make. You see a fly on the water, and you have seen a trout eat one of these flies, so you open your fly box and choose the one that's closest to the natural prey item. Make your selection in the following order and you should be in business:

1. *The size of the fly.* There is no need to measure the natural. Capture one if you can and place it on the lid of your fly box. If you cannot capture one, choose a fly that appears to be at least one size smaller than those

you see on the water and two sizes bigger than those in the air. Looks can be deceiving.

2. *The attitude and behavior of the fly on or in the water.* You can determine this by watching the insects hatch, by knowing something of their life history, or by observing the behavior of the trout. You'll see how to gauge all these later in the book. Check the insect's attitude on the surface. Is it flush with the surface film or riding high on the water? If you can determine this, you can choose either a high-floating fly or one that just barely hangs in the film. Check the natural's behavior. Is the insect fluttering across the surface or riding the currents sedately? If the insect is a nymph, is it drifting calmly with the currents or actively wiggling in the water column? With subsurface flies, you can get away with moving the imitation yourself. With flies on the surface, trying to make the fly twitch like a natural is a dangerous process because we invariably move the fly too much and cause drag. Although there are techniques to make a fly move, they require special flies, treating the leader, and positioning the fly precisely on the water. It's much more reliable to simulate movement by choosing a fly with lots of hackle, which causes an apparent illusion of movement, at least to the trout.

3. *The shape of the fly.* Is it a mayfly, caddisfly, or stonefly? Are the wings upright or sloped along the body? Is the natural long and skinny or short and squat?

4.   *The color of the fly.* Trout can see colors well, but their perception of color depends on lighting conditions and other factors beyond our understanding. A discussion of whether color makes a difference or not could fill an entire book. Experience shows that the most important factor is at least choosing the correct shade—if a trout is taking cream-colored flies, it often will reject a black one in favor of a tan or yellow one. Color is probably more important in subsurface flies than in high-floating dry flies.

3

A Quick Guide to Insect Identification

THE MOST ACCURATE WAY TO IDENTIFY, or key out, insects is with a binomial key, a type of "decision tree" in which you have two options for each anatomical characteristic. This, in turn, leads to choices between pairs of other characteristics. This is the way identifications are narrowed down in traditional entomology texts. However, I have found that people who are not familiar with scientific procedures have trouble with this approach. They prefer quick and easy charts. Look at the insect you are trying to identify—if it matches all of the characteristics in the chart below, you can be 90 percent sure of its identification.

Important Orders of Aquatic Insect Larvae

Insect	General Appearance
Mayfly Nymph 	Size: ⅛ to 1½ inches long. Color: tan, brown, cream, or olive. Shape: Anything from very skinny to broad and flattened. Found in all types of water.
Caddis Larva	Size: ¼ to 2 inches long. Color: Dull shade of cream, brown, olive, tan, yellow, or bright green. Shape: Caterpillar-like. Found in all types of water. Most larvae form cases made from stones, sticks, or other vegetation.
Caddis Pupa	Size: ¼ to 1¼ inches long. Color: dull. Shape: Distinctly curved. Found drifting in all types of water.

Important Orders of Aquatic Insect Larvae

Tails	Body
Thin and as long as the body of the insect. Two or three are present.	Feathery gills on abdomen may be apparent or almost invisible. Never has gills under thorax. Distinct wing pads on top of thorax.
None. A pair of tiny hooks are often present instead of tails.	Abdomen very fleshy and without gills. No wing pads present. Free-living caddisflies (ones that do not build cases) can be easily confused with aquatic beetle larvae, but examination with a hand lens shows that beetle larvae have distinct pincers around the mouth.
None.	Long trailing antennae. Emerging wings apparent and held close to body.

(Continued)

Important Orders of Aquatic Insect Larvae (Cont.)

Insect	General Appearance
Stonefly Nymph	Size: ½ to 2¼ inches long. Color: brown, black, tan, or yellow. Shape: Mostly flattened Nearly always found in fast water.
Midge Larva	Size: ⅟₃₂ to ⅜ inches long. Color: tan, brown, black, bright green, or red. Shape: Resemble tiny maggots Found in slow water.
Midge Pupa	Size: ⅟₃₂ to ⅜ inches long. Color: dull Shape: Curved with distinctly segmented abdomen. Found in slow water.

Important Orders of Aquatic Insect Larvae (Cont.)

Tails	Body
Always two, shorter than body length.	Gills located under thorax. Distinct antennae antennae and wing pads. Legs robust, each leg ends in two claws.
None, but a pair of tiny vestigial legs is visible at end of abdomen.	Eyes tiny. One pair of small prolegs at head.
None, but small feathery gills can often be seen at end of abdomen.	Wing pads tucked close to body. Distinct feathery gills branching off the front of the head. No long trailing antennae.

(Continued)

Important Orders of Aquatic Insect Larvae (Cont.)

Insect	Appearance at rest
Mayfly Dun (subimago)	Resembles a tiny sailboat. Wings always erect. Wings are speckled or translucent. Bodies full and opaque. Color: Varies from dark brown to bright pink.
Mayfly Spinner (imago, or adult)	Wings may be erect or prone on the surface of the water (in spent adults). Wings always transparent, sometimes with slight speckles. Bodies very skinny. Difficult to see on water when spent without close observation of the surface. Colors: Similar to those of duns.
Caddis Adult	Wings are tent-shaped and held low over body. Long, distinct antennae. No tails. Colors: Generally dull tan, brown, black, or gray.

Important Orders of Aquatic Insect Larvae (Cont.)

Appearance in the Air	Behavior
Look like tiny butterflies. Usually a distinct, cross-shaped profile. Only one pair of wings apparent.	Flutter or remain at rest on water. Stately, slow fliers. Usually fly upstream.
Tails distinct and longer than those of dun. Females can be seen with egg sacks. Only one pair of wings apparent.	Fast, agile fliers. Often seen in large mating swarms above the surface of the water. Will also form mating swarms over wet roads and shiny cars. Will be seen dipping and hovering over water. Emerged adults usually fly upstream.
Look like small moths when they fly. Only one pair of wings apparent.	Very active when hatching. Emerging adults often flutter and skitter across the water when hatching; they usually do not rest on water afterward. Quick fliers once they hatch. Usually fly upstream. Mating swarms fly upstream in long, continuous columns.

(Continued)

Important Orders of Aquatic Insect Larvae (Cont.)

Insect	Appearance at rest
Stonefly Adult	Wings always held flat over body. Adults look like nymphs with wings. Most hatch on rocks at the edge of streams unlike other aquatic insects.
Midge Adult	Resemble small mosquitoes. Long, spindly legs and feathery antennae. Distinct soft, fuzzy look. Wings held tight to body when at rest. Color: Usually black, gray, or cream.

Important Orders of Aquatic Insect Larvae (Cont.)

Appearance in the Air	Behavior
Two pairs of apparent wings. Heavy body usually seen hanging below wings in flight.	Slow, clumsy fliers. Will fly up or downstream. Only seen on the water when blown onto the surface after hatching or when returning to the water for mating flights. Females can be seen dipping into the water during mating flights.
Look like gnats or mosquitoes in the air.	Often skitter across the surface when hatching. Quick and agile fliers. Mating swarms form large groups just above the surface of the water. Individuals often clump together in twos or threes.

(Continued)

To choose a reasonable imitation of a natural that will allow you to catch trout, identifying insects on the stream as members of the correct scientific order—mayfly, caddisfly, stonefly, or midge—is probably as far as you need to go. If the trout are rising in midafternoon and you see a pinkish gray insect hatching at 3 o'clock, you can pick a fly from your box without knowing the species and still catch plenty of fish.

However, the ability to key an index to genus and species can tell you this bug is the mayfly Ephemerella subvaria, known to fly fishers as the Hendrickson. Now you can take advantage of some practical fishing tips.

Your fishing entomology text tells you that this particular mayfly forms big mating flights in the evening and that the insects fall to the water just after the sun sets, bringing large trout to the surface. Although you had a dinner date and were going to leave the water at 5 p.m., instead you stay until dark and have the best dry fly fishing of your life. You also have relationship difficulties for a few days.

This pocket-sized guide to streamside insect identification is not a fishing entomology guide, but the charts will help you identify the kind of insects you will commonly see trout eating. (I have limited these charts to the most important groups of aquatic insects and will assume that you can tell a grasshopper from a beetle.) The first chart will help you identify insect larvae that you will encounter by turning over rocks or placing a small aquarium net in the water.

4

How Do You Tell What They're Taking?

JUST KNOWING THERE ARE CREAM MAYflies on the water gray caddisflies in the air, or grasshoppers on the bank does not guarantee successful fishing, no matter how perfect your presentation. Catching trout consistently depends on a combination of proper presentation and a reasonable guess at what the trout are eating. Identifying the bug is only half the battle. For instance, even though the water is covered with adult mayflies, most of the trout may still be taking the nymphs under the surface. Or trout may pass up big juicy mayflies to sip mouthfuls of tiny midge pupae. You can learn a lot by observing how trout feed.

UNDERWATER

It's tough to tell what trout are feeding on when they are underwater. This is true in fast or deep water, dirty water, or in most rivers. Trout are well-camou-flaged, they seldom flash on their sides when feeding underwater (when you see this, it's usually suckers or whitefish), and they feed in places that make observa-tion difficult. If you can see a trout, so can an osprey or heron.

You usually can't see trout feeding below the surface when you are wading in a river, but if you can creep care-fully up to a deep bank or peer warily off the side of a bridge, you may be able to spot them. You can also spot trout feeding below the surface in late-season low water, and in the rich shallows of spring creeks and tailwater streams. Watch the fish carefully. A big school of fish is ei-ther a school of suckers, shad, or minnows, or else a bunch of trout that have been spooked and are hiding in the deepest water they can find. Trout don't normally school—anytime you see them close together, something is wrong.

A fish by itself or at least a few feet from another one might be feeding. A fish that is motionless for up to five minutes is resting, spooked, or just plain not eating. You have no clues. A fish that darts from side to side without tipping upward is eating some type of larvae or crustaceans close to the bottom. A fish that tips up for food is eating emerging insects, particularly if the fish occasionally breaks the surface in a swirl.

Generally, the larger the insect, the farther a trout will move to intercept it. Trout will move two feet for a size 8 Green Drake nymph, but will seldom move more than six inches for a midge larva. Some larvae, like those of damselflies, a few species of mayflies, and some caddisflies, can swim quickly. Trout will run down and capture these insects with a long pursuit instead of just making a quick dart to one side.

If you see a big swirl—one that looks as if a trout just made a quick 90-degree turn—that often indicates a trout that is chasing minnows. If you see this after dark in the moonlight, at first light, or if the water has just risen with a sudden rainstorm, you can be even more certain.

Although trout rarely grub right on the bottom of rivers, generally letting the current bring the food to them instead, once in a while you'll see trout bottom feed in an unusual manner. Sometimes trout will work their snouts under rocks to pry caddisfly cases from the bottom. I once saw a trout root a big crayfish out from under a flat rock. In spring creeks, trout sometimes shake weeds the way a puppy shakes a rag, then drop back to gulp the scuds and sowbugs they have shaken loose.

By watching a trout feed underwater, you can make an educated guess as to the size of their food, whether it swims or not, and where it is drifting in the water column. All these observations can help you narrow down the right fly pattern.

Turning over rocks on the bottom of the river or grabbing a handful of submerged vegetation and spreading it out on the shore can help you figure out what the fish may be eating. Crustaceans, such as scuds and sowbugs, never hatch, so unless you look under the surface, you'll never see them. When looking for insects under rocks, pick flat rocks in shallow water with a fast to moderate current. Most insects hatch in riffles, and the species that are about to hatch, which are more available to the fish, will often migrate to the shallows before hatching.

ON THE SURFACE

A hatch of aquatic insects, even one that seems to cover the water surface, does not always guarantee rising trout. Trout may be eating tiny or spent insects when all you see are big ones. This can frustrate you unless you stop, relax, and observe both the trout and the surface of the water. If you see trout rising, watch the water for about five minutes before you jump in. Watch the slow backwaters along the bank for insects. You can even see nymphs drifting below the surface if the water is clear enough and you look carefully. If you can't see anything along the banks, wade out to a place where trout aren't rising, so you won't spoil the water by frightening them. Bend down close to the water and wait. Close all your pockets and take off your hat before you bend down really close to the water. Look now, and you can often see tiny mayflies or spent insects that were invisible from the bank.

Once you have spotted the insects riding the surface, try to figure out which ones the trout are taking. The luckiest situation is when trout are eating the juicy mayflies with big sailboat wings that you see twitching on the surface. Right—fat chance. It's seldom so easy.

You often can't see anything disappear into the mouth of a trout when it is rising. So if the trout isn't eating a big insect with upright wings, your other choices are tiny insects on the surface, spent insects in the surface film, or emerging insects just below the surface.

It's fairly easy to tell when a trout is taking an insect below the surface. When a trout takes an insect within inches of the surface, the momentum of its rise to feed brings the fish through the film, or at least the swirl the feeding trout makes carries through to the surface. Sometimes subsurface feeding can produce a hefty splash. But if you look carefully, you won't see any big bubbles.

When a trout takes an insect from the surface it also takes in air, expelling the air from its gills as it swallows. In general, the bigger the splash accompanying the rise, the more likely it is that the fish fed just below the surface.

Your clue to a trout eating insects on the surface is either big bubbles trailing the rise form or seeing the trout's snout poke through the film. The snout may also be followed slowly by the dorsal fin and even a wiggle of the tail. A violent, noisy rise can mean either a trout going after an insect twitching across the surface or a big one. A sedate rise with most of the head and dorsal fin breaching the surface like a miniature porpoise often means the trout is eating a spent insect such as a mayfly spinner or ovipositing, or egg-laying, caddis. A quiet rise that is more concentric and just shows the snout of the fish is usually the end of a tiny mayfly or midge.

IN THE AIR

The first insects we notice when walking toward a trout stream are the ones in the air—especially if they are trying to bite us. They may be helpful, but they can also be misleading. Slow-moving insects that rise from the water's surface and quickly head for streamside brush have just hatched and are good clues for fly selection. Insects hovering over the water and dipping on its surface are laying eggs. They will soon fall to the surface as spent adults and are also worth a close look. However, flying insects that move upstream in a rush, like commuters leaving a subway terminal, may only be migrating. If so, they might not touch the surface of the water for days. These huge insect flights, most often seen with caddisflies and midges, can be frustrating—so many insects and not one available to the trout!

Trout can't eat insects that are in the air. (That's not entirely true—small trout sometimes leap into the air for insects hovering above the water.) You might see massive clouds of mayfly spinners above the water, but they could be mating and perhaps not a single one has touched the water yet. The trout could be rising, but they might be rising for an entirely different insect—one that's hatching at or near the surface. So insects in the air are only a clue, not necessarily the answer.

The best way to spot insects in the air is to look into the sun. You can miss a cloud of tiny mayflies unless you see sunlight reflecting off their wings. Another way to spot them is to look against a dark-colored bank or tree. Look just above the water first, but then keep looking up. Eastern Green Drake spinners can form mating flights one hundred feet above the water. If you spot them early, you can watch them gradually descend to the water and be prepared with the right fly when they finally land on the surface, usually just at dark.

Insects are attracted to shiny surfaces and apparently get fooled into thinking wet pavement or car windshields are water. I live about one hundred yards from a trout stream, yet I can tell when mayfly spinners are active by watching them dip above my windshield in the driveway.

5

Mayflies

THIS BOOK IS NOT A FIELD GUIDE TO KEY-
ing aquatic insects to genus and species. Scores of great
references are available, should you find the need to learn
how to identify aquatic insects better. Knowing exactly
which insect is on the water can be helpful, though, because once you have identified an insect, you can benefit
from the efforts of a century of other people who have
tried to imitate that specific bug. Nonetheless, for practical fishing, if you can catch a sample of the hatch and
identify an insect to its scientific order (for instance, mayflies are classified as the order Ephemeroptera and caddisflies are Tricoptera), you'll be able to pick a fly that will
match the hatch and catch trout. If you learn to suspect
when trout are feeding on prey other than insects, such as
leeches, scuds, or sculpins, and know which flies imitate
them, you can make an educated guess about which fly
to use.

LIFE HISTORY

The order Ephemeroptera—named for the fleeting lifespan of the insects in this group—is an ancient and primitive group of insects. An individual mayfly's lifespan is almost exactly twelve months; as with most aquatic insects, most of that life cycle (about eleven months and twenty-nine days) is spent as an aquatic larva or nymph. Short-lived adult females lay eggs on the surface of the water. The eggs fall into spaces between pebbles on the bottom of the river, or come to rest in aquatic vegetation. The nymphs hatch in a few days and then spend their time in vegetation, under rocks, or burrowing in sand and silt. The nymphs—a significant source of trout food—are most available to trout during periods of nocturnal drift or when adults are hatching.

When the nymphs mature and water temperatures are right, the wing pads on the thorax turn dark. If you collect a small sample from the bottom of a river that includes mayfly nymphs at this stage, this is one way to tell which insects are about to hatch. The nymphs begin to drift and rise to the surface, where they split their nymphal shuck and emerge as duns, or subimagos—an immature winged adult form unique to mayflies. This hatching takes place over a period ranging from minutes to hours in any given day, and hatches of particular species can last for a few days to a few weeks each season.

The duns dry their wings and fly to streamside foliage. They rest in the shade for a day or two, molt one final time into the mature adult stage, and return to the corridor above the water surface to mate, lay eggs, and die.

The mature adults, called spinners or imagos, form clouds over the surface. Their rhythmic mating dance is distinctive and cannot be mistaken for that of any other insect. Typically, adult mayflies fly upstream in a deliberate procession, then stop and dip in a pattern distinctive to each species. You will most often see them dip over broken water. Males intercept females midair and fertilize the eggs, which can often be seen as bright orange or green balls at the end of the females' abdomens. The males then fall to the water and die, while the females lay the eggs by dipping their abdomens on the surface, dropping a trail of eggs in a dive-bombing run or, less frequently, by crawling underwater and depositing the eggs on aquatic plants. Then, like the males, the females are off, lying spent on the surface until they sink to the bottom.

IMPORTANT STAGES

Mayflies are the most important source of trout food in many streams. There are hundreds of species throughout the world. In any given stream in North America, you might see several to dozens of different species during the course of a year. Trout seem to relish all stages in a mayfly's life cycle. Mayfly nymphs form the bulk of the trout's diet, because they are available to trout twelve months a year. However, when adult mayflies are hatching, trout will consume huge quantities of them because the flies are so abundant. In fact, a trout may obtain more than 50 percent of its calories for the year during the few months when mayflies are hatching. Binge feeding can be a successful life strategy for a fish.

When mayflies are hatching and trout are rising, it's tempting to fish a high-floating dry fly. After all, most of us enjoy seeing fish grab a dry fly from the surface. But if you want to play the percentages, you'll catch more fish by using an emerger. This can be anything from a fly designed to ride just below the surface film to a regular old dry fly without flotant or with most of its hackle trimmed off. Trout know that a live mayfly dun riding on its tip-toes will soon fly away, and if they commit to rising for a fully emerged adult, they might come up empty. Emerging mayflies, though, are more helpless prey; they spend a lot of time splitting their nymphal shuck while attempting to penetrate the surface film, which presents a tough barrier.

Spinners, though, are a different story and are actually a better life stage to imitate for the person who likes to fish floating flies. Trout know that a spinner, or spent adult, is not going anywhere once it hits the water. This is one of the few times that a dry fly will catch more trout than a fly just below the surface.

Mayflies hatch from March to November in most streams. East of the Mississippi, their emergence is concentrated in May and June; in the Rockies and West Coast mountains most of them emerge in June and July. One genus, Baetis, may hatch all winter in tailwater streams or spring creeks. Mayflies are creatures of cold, highly oxygenated water. They are more common in the upper and middle reaches of trout streams, but silt-dwelling species can be found in lower, warmer, muddier reaches of some trout waters—in fact, these insects can be found in warmer water than trout can tolerate.

Typically, mayfly populations will be more diverse in clear rocky streams. In spring creeks, lakes, and tailwaters, mayflies are abundant but often restricted to one or two species, usually the smaller species in running water and sometimes giant mayflies like the size 6 Hexagenia in lakes. This can make your life easier, because you only have to worry about using a few fly patterns.

On a daily basis, trout feed on nymphs all day if some species are hatching. But even if there aren't any hatching, trout feed heavily on nymphs in the morning. In the early and late season, when the water temperatures are below 50 degrees Fahrenheit, mayflies hatch during the warmest part of the day, from noon to 4 p.m. In the middle of the season, mayflies can hatch all day long, with hatching times gradually shifting toward the evening hours as the weather gets warmer. In the hottest part of summer, you'll find more mayfly duns in the morning than in the evening.

Spinners typically congregate and mate in the evening, especially east of the Mississippi. In the higher altitudes of the Rockies, however, you might find more spinners at midday. These spinner flights are often brief, heavy, and seem to depend on air temperature. For example, in trout streams of the Catskills and other eastern rivers, in early May you will see spinner flights from 3 to 6 p.m. As the weather warms, you may not see any spinners until the sun leaves the water. And as air temperatures hit daily highs of 80 degrees Fahrenheit, you probably will not see any spinners on the water until dark when their flights last well into the night.

SOME IMPORTANT SPECIES

If you've never fished a mayfly hatch, it's helpful to know about a few specific types to get an idea of what to expect. The following are just samples of the mayflies you might find, but I have tried to choose those considered the most important to trout and fly fishers. There are many other species in most trout streams; you may wish to consult other books to help identify them.

Blue-Winged Olive (various Baetis species). These tiny insects are the most abundant mayfly in many rivers, particularly those with some weed growth. They are common in trout waters throughout the world. Unlike other species, Blue-Winged Olives are supposedly multi-brooded and produce several hatches in a twelve-month period. The nymphs are small, from a size 16 to 22; they are also slim in appearance and can swim, though not as well as minnow mayflies, such as the Isonychia. They are olive-brown in color with delicate, almost invisible legs. A Pheasant Tail nymph is a nearly perfect imitation of a Baetis mayfly, particularly in an olive color. Because these mayflies are multibrooded, there are always some nymphs in the water, so they can be fished year-round. Use a dead drift with an occasional twitch for the most effective tactic.

The Baetis dun is also important as a trout food item. It hatches particularly well on cloudy and rainy days. Typically, the flies start hatching in late morning and keep hatching until late afternoon. Experienced fly fishers often hope for a nasty day in April, even one that spits snow, as perfect timing for a heavy Baetis hatch. The duns have an olive-brown body with gray wings. An emerger works better than a high-floating dry for this hatch, unless you see fish actually taking the duns from the surface.

The nymph stage of the Blue-Winged Olive. Note the skinny legs and tails.

The Blue-Winged Olive dun is one of the most abundant mayflies in the world.

The spinners are not as important as the duns or nymphs, because they sometimes fall on evenings when the water temperature drops too low to stimulate trout feeding or when the water is too high and fast for trout to notice the spinners hitting the water. However, I have had great fishing with Baetis spinners in September, when the water is low and warm enough for trout to spot these tiny insects. The spinners are brown with clear wings. A Rusty Spinner in the appropriate size is a great imitation.

Hendrickson (Ephemerella subvaria). This mayfly—known to fly fishers as the Hendrickson—may be the most famous American mayfly. It hatches only east of the Mississippi in rocky, gravelly streams and is seldom found in spring creeks. It is often the first hatch of the season to bring trout to the surface, starting in mid-April in southern Appalachian streams and as late as early June in the Adirondacks and Maine. There is no mistaking a Hendrickson hatch, because the insects almost always hatch in great numbers within a short time.

The nymphs are brownish olive with distinct legs and tails. The wing pads become very dark a few days before these mayflies hatch. A size 14 Hendrickson or Hare's Ear nymph will work when trout are eating the nymphs. Fishing a nymph before the hatch is sometimes productive but not always reliable, as high water might make it difficult to get your nymph down low enough to trout feeding near the bottom.

Hendrickson nymphs are found in fast water with small rocks and gravel.

Make sure you use a weighted fly and put some weight on the leader if you fish nymphs.

Duns are fat and juicy-looking, with pinkish bodies, sometimes tinged with olive. The wings are medium gray. Duns will hatch at nearly the same time each day, typically between 2 and 3 p.m. Unlike many other mayflies, these insects hatch best on sunny days. Once you see a Hendrickson dun on the water, get your fly and leader ready, because the hatch will last for an hour and a half at most. Hendrickson duns spend a lot of time on the water drying their wings. Trout and birds take advantage of this trait and so can you. As with most mayfly hatches, an emerger will

The Hendrickson spinner provides great sport on warm spring evenings.

work best at the beginning and sometimes through the hatch, but toward the end all the flies on the water may be fully emerged duns. Trout will key on these. By cocktail time, you'll never know there were mayflies on the water.

Anglers who leave the river after the hatch may miss the spinner falls entirely. Insects that have hatched over the past few days will form large mating flights and fall to the water within a few minutes of each other, driving trout into a feeding frenzy for about thirty minutes. Many fishermen prefer the spinner falls of this insect to the more famous dun hatches. The spinners seem to bring the large trout to the surface—fish that seldom bother with floating insects. Spinners might fall in midafternoon on cool, clear days, but once the air temperature hits the 70s during the afternoon, the spinners do not start to fall until the sun leaves the water. During periods of cool, windy, or rainy weather, spinners might not fall for several days. However, you will see the spinners migrating and massing over riffles for hours before they actually fall on the water, which will give you lots of time to get ready. Hendrickson spinners are rusty red with distinct rings on their abdomens. Wings are clear, and females carry bright yellow egg sacks.

Eastern March Brown (Stenonema vicarium). This is a mayfly that produces better nymph fishing than dry fly fishing. Strictly an eastern mayfly, it hatches from mid-May until early June. As soon as you see lilacs and apple blossoms, the March Browns, named for an English mayfly that actually does hatch in March, will be a few days behind. The nymphs are large and flattened with robust legs and tails. They are a mottled brownish tan and can be seen scuttling for safety when you pick up flat rocks. Because of their shape, they must live in fast water where they can hide under big rocks; you won't find them in spring creeks or rivers composed mostly of sand or fine gravel. Nymphs spend most of the year hidden under rocks, but a few days prior to hatching they migrate into the shallows, where they are exposed to the ravages of feeding trout. A nymph that imitates a March Brown larva fished from dawn to midmorning in fast, rocky water will produce big trout, often in large numbers. Luck-

March Brown duns are large and meaty, but trout often ignore them.

ily, the nymphs are not hard to imitate; a size 10 through 14 Hare's Ear or March Brown nymph will take any trout looking for these morsels. (March Browns are a size 10, but there are several smaller Stenonema species that are similar in coloration and behavior.)

The March Brown duns are huge for mayflies, stately, and take a long time to dry their wings and get off the water. The duns have a dark brown abdomen that is creamy underneath and wings that are speckled with black and brown. The wings slant back over the body more so than in other mayflies. March Browns usually hatch from early morning until about 11 a.m., and may hatch again in the evening. Unfortunately, trout seem to be wary of taking so big a fly on nice days. You can watch thousands of beautiful duns drift through a pool and perhaps see one eight-inch fish splash at one. However, if the water rises from a storm and gets dirty, or if you see March Browns hatching on a drizzly day, trout may be all over the duns. Nonetheless, seeing many trout taking March Brown duns is a rare event.

The big March Brown spinner appears at dusk.

March Brown spinners can give you better fishing than the duns, perhaps because they fall just at dark, when trout seem to be less wary. The spinners are big, with a tan body and clear wings that have pale speckles. They fly straight upstream and make long, vertical dips. You don't always see their mating flights until right before dark, so sometimes they can catch you by surprise. Many of the fly-fishing entomology texts say March Brown spinners are not important as trout food, but in New York and New England, I have found the spinners to produce more consistent surface activity in trout than the duns.

Pale Evening Dun, Pale Morning Dun (various Ephemerella and Drunella species). This is a group of important small, cream-colored mayflies that have similar behavior and nearly identical fly patterns. In the West, they hatch in late morning, usually from 11 a.m. to 2 p.m.; in the East, they hatch just before dark and into twilight. These duns are some of the most abundant yet frustrating bugs on trout streams. They bring large numbers of trout to the surface, but the number of times you connect with them might be disappointing unless your presentation and fly pattern are perfect. Luckily, the nymphs are easier to imitate. Use a Hare's Ear for the

The Pale Morning Dun nymph is a shape and color that is shared by a number of mayfly species.

The Pale Morning Dun is perhaps the best mayfly hatch in the Rocky Mountains.

The Pale Evening Dun of the East is similar to the Pale Morning Dun but hatches right at dark.

larger varieties (sizes 14 and 16) and a Pheasant Tail for the smaller ones (sizes 18 to 22); these flies will catch trout quite easily an hour before the hatch.

Once the duns begin to hatch, you will notice they leave the water swiftly unless it's raining. Because of this, trout seem to select the emergers and will often ignore a standard dry fly floating high with its wings erect. Duns have light-colored bodies that show tinges of cream, olive, yellow, and sometimes orange. The shade varies with species and water chemistry. Wings can be pale yellow, cream, or pale gray. Try to match the natural as closely as possible in size and color, and use an emerger rather than a dun unless you are sure you see fish taking the winged adults. Trim a standard dry fly if you have to.

Spinners are light brown with clear wings. The western ones return to the water at midday; the eastern ones fall right at dark. This is another spinner that does not get much attention from the fly-fishing insect books, but it is one I have found to bring trout to the surface consistently. A Rusty spinner will imitate them well enough to fool the trout.

Tricos (various Tricorythodes species). Tricos are the most important hatch of late summer and early fall and may be the only mayfly hatch of significance in August and September. They are among the tiniest of mayflies, but the spinners fall in vast numbers within a short time, usually less than an hour. Tricos are found throughout

Trico duns hatch in the evening or early morning.

North America and are one of the most widely distrib-
uted mayflies. The nymphs live in silty water that won't
support any other mayfly species; slow water with a soft
bottom supports the most abundant populations. Silt can
be found in small pockets even in riffled water, however,
and you are likely to encounter Tricos in almost any kind
of stream except for rocky headwaters.

Few anglers fish imitations of these nymphs, but a tiny
Pheasant Tail (size 20 or 22) will fool trout just before the
duns emerge in late evening or early morning. In western
rivers, they seem to hatch more often in the evening,
whereas in eastern rivers you're more likely to see them

at dawn. Duns have a gray or dirty cream body with pale gray wings and a pronounced black thorax. They are often ignored by anglers looking for the flashier spinners, but the duns can add another dimension to summer fishing and extend your productive hours on the water. You will find them hatching in slow water, as well as fast water below slow pools. A tiny Adams or virtually any small fly will work, so long as it is the right size.

Duns molt quickly into spinners, and sometimes the duns that hatched at dawn will fall as spinners a few hours later. Spinners form huge mating flights that are difficult to see unless you look into the sun. The male spinners have dark brown abdomens and a thick black thorax. Wings and tails are long and clear. Females look the same, but their abdomens are cream or pale green. Migrating clouds will zigzag upstream, and when they find an appropriate riffle, thousands of spinners will form tight balls about twenty feet above the water. This ball will slowly descend and spinners will fall to the water when the air temperature hits exactly 68 degrees Fahrenheit, an interesting tidbit discovered by Jim McClennan, a noted authority on angling on Alberta's Bow River. Spinners fall in such great numbers that trout feed incessantly, taking as many insects as they can in a short time.

Despite the small size of these insects, fishing can be relatively easy for the late season. I have approached trout feeding on Trico spinners and have been able to touch them with my rod tip. The main problem during Trico hatches is getting trout to notice your fly among the thousands of naturals. If the water is carpeted with spinners, try fishing a fly slightly bigger than the ones you see—trout may think your fly is a group of spinners clumped together—or try a small ant or beetle.

Western Green Drake (various species of the genus Drunella). These are some of the largest and most exciting mayflies to hatch in western rivers. There are about a half-dozen related species that look similar and hatch in the same manner. The bigger flies—sizes 10 and 12—hatch first in June and July. The smaller species—sizes 14 and 16—hatch from late June through early September. Nymphs are robust and slightly flattened; they live in medium-fast water. They are olive-brown in color, and a Hare's Ear nymph in olive is a great imitation. Fish the nymph a few hours before these flies begin hatching.

Duns hatch around midday and are the most important stage of this insect. All species have dark gray wings and bodies that are brownish olive on top and yellow-green on the bottom. They are distinctly ringed. As with most mayfly hatches, an emerger is your best bet, especially in the early parts of the hatch when nymphs are struggling against the surface film. Green Drake duns take a long time to dry their wings, however, and trout may become selective to fully emerged insects. This hatch

The Green Drake dun is eagerly anticipated by western fly fishers because it is the first big mayfly of the season.
Ross Purnell

can be condensed into a short time and you should be ready to fish any time from 11 a.m. to 3 p.m. Once you see duns on the water, you might have only thirty minutes of dry fly action. Trout get selective to this insect, so it's best to have a dry fly designed specifically for Green Drake duns.

Spinners aren't nearly as important as the duns. They fall in the evening, sometimes into dark, but seldom fall in numbers concentrated enough to get trout interested in coming to the surface. Still, if you carry the ubiquitous

Rusty spinner in sizes 12 through 16, you'll be ready in case you do find trout feeding on Green Drake spinners.

SUGGESTED FLY PATTERNS

There is a temptation to buy or tie a different pattern for each species of mayfly. This strategy will drive you nuts (and broke!). Most popular dry flies will imitate scores of species of mayflies. For instance, although the Gray Fox dry fly was designed to imitate one species, Stenonema fuscum, it is a perfect imitation for a dozen species of Stenonema mayflies—bugs with common names, such as the March Brown, Light Cahill, and Ginger Quill. Following is a list of suggested flies that will be successful throughout the country. In many cases, I have listed generic descriptions. To imitate the Hendrickson mayfly, you can choose between CDC Emergers, Soft Hackle Emergers, Thorax Dries, No Hackle Dries, Parachute Dries, and scores of others. Pick one that looks good to you, or ask the person in the fly shop which one works best in your local waters.

The Hare's Ear nymph imitates many species of mayflies.

Fly Patterns: Nymphs

Pattern	Sizes	Region and Season
Pheasant Tail	12, 14, 16, 18, 20	All regions, all season.
Gold-Ribbed Hare's Ear	8, 10, 12, 14, 16, 18	April–October in all regions.
Zug Bug	10, 12, 14	June–September in all regions.
Eastern March Brown	10, 12, 14	May–June in the East.
Hendrickson	12, 14	May in the East.
Callibaetis	12, 14, 16	West, mainly in lakes and spring creeks.
Lepage's Bead-Head Mayfly	12, 14, 16	May–July in all regions.

Fly Patterns: Dries and Emergers

Pattern	Sizes	Region and Season
Blue-Winged Olive	18, 20, 22	All of North America, all season long, but especially in March–April and September–October.
Hendrickson	12, 14, 16	April–May in the East.
Pale Morning Dun or Pale Evening Dun	14, 16, 18, 20	May–August in the West. May–June in the East.
Gray Fox	10, 12, 14, 16	May–June in the East.
Callibaetis	12, 14, 16	June–August in the West.
Western Green Drake	12, 14, 16	June–July in the West.
Coffin Fly	10, 12	May–June in the East.
Dun Variant	10, 12, 14	June–September in all regions.
Rusty spinner	12, 14, 16, 18, 20	April–August in all regions.
Olive spinner	14, 16, 18	June–July in all regions.
Trico spinner	18, 20, 22, 24	August–September in all regions.
Adams	10, 12, 14, 16, 18, 20	May–October in all regions.

FISHING STRATEGIES

Dead drift. Dead drift. Dead drift. Yes, mayflies do flutter, and some of the nymphs can swim, but for 95 percent of the mayfly hatches you encounter, the best fishing will be had by making the fly drift naturally with the current. Most of the twitches we impart to flies, especially dry flies, are far too overt to imitate the delicate flutter of a live dun or spinner. You can get away with twitching a nymph during a hatch to catch a trout's attention and imitate the struggling nymph, but again, keep these maneuvers subtle and to a minimum. Exceptions to this rule are the Callibaetis mayfly, usually found in ponds, and the Isonychia mayfly, found in streams, both of which are agile swimmers. If in your search of the shallows you see large mayflies that swim like minnows, fish your nymphs with fast strips.

Fish mayfly nymphs deep in the morning, in cold water, and in fast water. This means using a weighted fly, a Bead-Head pattern, or putting weight onto your leader. You'll know you have enough weight if the fly occasionally hangs up on the bottom. A strike indicator is often useful in detecting strikes and to suspend your fly at the right level. As you begin to see mayflies emerging during the day, and if you see periodic rises, switch to an unweighted nymph. As rises become more frequent, switch to an emerger and fish it just in or under the surface film.

The classic Hendrickson dry fly with its full hackle is only one of many imitations of the Hendrickson dun.

You might want to fish the emerger right through the hatch, but if you start to see trout plucking duns from the water, fish a high-floating dry fly with upright wings.

When you see spinners in the air, check the surface to make sure some are actually falling to the water. Once you are sure the spinners are falling, fish a dry fly with upright wings if you see their wings. If the flies are lying spent with their wings in the film, you will have to switch to a spent dry fly. If you don't have a spent spinner, pick a dry fly that's closest in size and color to the naturals. Trim the hackles and wings on the top and bottom of the fly with a pair of scissors. Sometimes just crushing a fly into a spent shape with your fingers will work.

After trout stop rising to the spinners, which is usually after dark, switch to a wet fly or nymph approximately the size and shape of the spinners, and fish it swung in the current to imitate a drowned spinner.

6

Caddisflies

IN MANY RIVERS, ESPECIALLY FAST, ROCKY tailwater rivers, such as Montana's Madison or California's Pit River, caddisflies, also known as sedges, outnumber mayflies and outrank them as trout food. Most are drab in color and don't offer the brilliant spectrum mayflies do, but the shape of caddisflies and their diverse behavior when hatching and laying eggs make it important that you understand their life cycle and behavior. Customary techniques for fishing mayfly hatches often don't work with caddisflies.

LIFE HISTORY

Caddisflies also have a twelve-month life cycle but typically spend more time as winged adults than mayflies. Caddisfly larvae are a diverse and fascinating group. Most species build themselves cases from particular sizes and shapes of sticks or stones. The cases protect the larvae and serve as ballast to keep them from being swept away. Caddis larvae in slow water or in lakes usually build cases out of twigs and actively crawl across the bottom, where they are picked up by trout. Caddis larvae in fast water often attach themselves to rocks with their anterior claws or by forming barnacle-like cases that cling to the undersides of rocks. A few species of caddis are called free-living because they don't build cases. Others construct elaborate nets to capture food and keep from being washed away.

Caddis pupae are the stage favored by trout because they are easy to capture.

Unlike mayflies, caddisflies have a complete meta-morphosis, which includes a pupal stage. From a week to a month before hatching, caddis larvae change into the pupal stage, sealing themselves into cocoons that are either free-standing or within their cases. Turn over a few rocks in a riffle and inspect the caddis cases you find. If the larva pokes itself out of the case, that species will not be hatching soon. If the cases are sealed but you can feel something inside, those species are due to hatch. You might wish to break one open to see the color and size of the pupa. Pupae have a tightly coiled body and embryonic wings, seen as pads held under the body of the insect. When emerging, the pupae burst from the cocoons. Some drift helplessly in the current, like mayfly nymphs, but many pop quickly to the surface, like a balloon held under water. Other free-living caddis swim briskly through the current and across the surface before hatching.

Caddis adults look like moths and are very active on the water.

Although a caddisfly may drift a long way as a pupa, once it is ready to hatch the adult breaks its pupal skin and leaves the water, usually more quickly than a mayfly does. Some caddisfly species may have trouble getting airborne if it's cold or raining, but the typical caddisfly behavior is for the adult to take to the air immediately or make a couple hops on the surface and then fly away quickly. Caddisfly wings dry within the pupal case, so they don't need to dry after hatching as in mayflies.

Unlike mayflies, caddisflies may live up to a month before mating, laying eggs, and dying. They often migrate by forming huge flights that dominate the air above a trout stream for hours and days on end. Anglers see clouds of caddisflies in the air, but what they don't realize is that not one insect is hitting the water unless a stray gust of wind blows one to the surface. Adults spend their days hidden along streamside brush where males and females mate. You can find out what kinds of caddisflies are present by shaking streamside bushes. However, you won't see the water covered with rising trout until the females return to the water to lay eggs. You can tell when the adult females are actually on the water by looking at the surface carefully. Watch for insects dive bombing the surface and bouncing on it—or look at your waders. Your waders? Yes—many species of caddisflies, particularly the little gray ones, swim underwater and onto rocks and logs in the river, depositing their eggs on these obstructions.

You'll see these kinds on your waders just above and below the waterline.

IMPORTANT STAGES

Trout regularly eat caddis larvae, but only certain types are available to them on a daily basis. Larvae that stay trapped within nets they build on submerged rocks and the species that form round stone cases seldom get into the drift unless flood waters are strong enough to tear them loose. However, one genus of caddis larva, Ryacophila, is a free-living, predatory larva that moves constantly along the stream bottom. Known as Green Rockworms, these larvae can be the most important source of food to trout that live in riffled water. Another caddis larva, genus Brachycentrus, forms tube-shaped cases, but these larvae move constantly along the stream bottom and often get swept away and eaten by trout. A third larva, genus Hydropsyche, is a net spinner, which strains organic matter from the current.

It's ironic that most of the flies sold to imitate caddisflies are imitations of the high-riding adult insect, the least important stage to trout. In the past twenty years, though, far more attention has been paid to caddis pupae, especially since the publication of Gary La-Fontaine's landmark book, *Caddisflies* (1981). Because adult insects fly away so quickly, experienced adult trout have learned to concentrate on the pupae. Think about it—in between an insect that stays hidden on the bottom of a river and one that flies away quickly is a life stage that drifts underwater for a long time and has trouble breaking through the surface film.

Egg-laying females can be almost as important as pupae. They may bounce on the water, dive into the water and swim under to lay eggs, or crawl into the water from rocks along the bank. Look on the surface to be sure they're actually getting onto the water, check your waders, or put a small handnet into the water to see if any drowned adults are drifting in the current. Trout may eat these insects as they lie spent on the surface, as they swim underwater, or they may pick up the drowned ones that have already laid their eggs.

Caddis larva imitations can be fished all year long, but they are especially effective from May through September. Caddis larvae are more common in riffles than slow pools and are far more abundant in rocky streams than weedy spring creeks. The best time and place to fish caddis larvae is early in the morning in the fastest water you can find.

Caddis pupae always ring the dinner bell for trout because they are the most vulnerable stage in a caddisfly's life cycle. Early in the hatch, caddis pupae are drifting deep along the bottom, but as the hatch progresses and you begin to see adult caddis in the air, pupae drifting just under the surface will be more important to trout. There are few trout streams that don't have caddis pupae emerging at some time of the day throughout the spring, summer, and fall. They are most abundant in the morning and evening during summer, but in May you will find most of them in the middle of the day. You often won't see caddis pupae unless you look carefully in the water. Your first tip will be adult caddis rising from the surface. The second will be that trout are ignoring your standard dry fly or refusing it with a splash. Because most caddis larvae live in riffles, most pupae will be found emerging in riffles, too. But because pupae can drift a long distance before emerging, you may also find them in slower water. Unlike most mayflies, caddisflies emerge all day long, often from dawn to well after dark. This keeps trout interested all day, but it might be difficult for you to figure out what the fish are taking.

Recently emerged caddis adults can also be important trout food. Especially when the water is cold or during rainstorms, the adults can't get airborne as quickly as usual, and trout will sip them eagerly. On windy days, gusts will blow the adults back into the water where lucky trout inhale them. Additionally, because adults live in streamside brush for up to a month, they are constantly falling into the water; trout living close to the bank will be on the lookout for caddis that tumble into the water. You'll see this most often in the middle of the day when the wind picks up. A few types of adult caddis skitter along the surface after they've hatched and trout will often key into this behavior. It will be apparent when this is happening, as rises to these adults will be vicious slashes.

Egg-laying females return to the water at any time of day, but mostly in the evening. Calm, clear, warm evenings will be the best. At the first sign of wind or rain, the adults will head back to their shelter in the bushes and try again when conditions improve. Most caddis lay eggs in riffles, so look for them in fast water first. A number of species lay their eggs in slower water, however, so don't rule out flats and slow pools if you see caddis adults in the air. Because caddis can live for a month after hatching but conditions are not always right for laying eggs, these flights of egg-laying females can be massive and sometimes blanket the air and the water. Such an evening might be the high point of your fishing season.

SOME IMPORTANT SPECIES

Unlike mayflies, caddisflies are difficult to identify, and most of them look similar. Consequently, common names and specific fly patterns for these insects are rare. The

most important groups of caddisflies can be lumped together because their appearance and behavior are similar.

Black Caddis (Brachycentrus, and other genera).
There are many species of caddisfly adults that fit the
same description—dark gray almost black wings, dark
green body, size 14 or 16. The famous Mother's Day
Caddis of the Rocky Mountains, the early season Black
Caddis of the Midwest, and the Grannom or Shad Fly of
the Catskills and New England can all be lumped into
this group. Larvae form four-sided, slim cases of vegeta-
ble debris from the bottom of the river. Pupae emerge in
the morning or early afternoon in slower water than
most other caddisflies. The adults ride the water longer
than most and can provide surface action rivaling that of
many mayfly species. The egg-laying females return to
the water in late afternoon through the evening. Larvae
are imitated by a small Hare's Ear nymph or a generic
cased caddis imitation. Flies to imitate the pupae are the
LaFontaine Deep pupa and LaFontaine Emerging pupa
in gray or dark green or a small dark Bead-Head Caddis.
Adults are best imitated by a Black Elk Hair Caddis. Fish
taking egg-laying adults will rise to a Dark Gray CDC or
Spent Caddis imitation, and drowned adults will be best
imitated by a small wet fly, such as a Gold-Ribbed Hare's
Ear.

The distinctive case of the Black Caddis.

The Little Black Caddis is found throughout the country.

Speckled Sedge (Hydropsyche species). Although these net spinners can be found in all rocky trout waters, they concentrate in tailwaters because of their ability to strain plankton from the water. (Plankton does not exist in free-running streams.) In most tailwaters, the larvae are so abundant that some are always drifting in the current, especially early in the morning. Pupae rise to the surface quickly and emerge from late afternoon until after dark.

The Speckled Sedge is abundant in tailwater rivers.

The adults have tan or light green bodies, and the wings are light brown with strong black speckles. This is one of those frustrating species in which the adults pop quickly from the pupal shuck and spend little time on the water. Compounding this difficulty are the egg-laying females, which return to the water at the same time pupae are hatching. The females swim underwater to lay their eggs and then rise back to the surface where they get swept away. Needless to say, if you see these insects when trout are rising, you are better off fishing a fly just under the surface than a high-floating dry. Larvae are imitated with a Green or Tan Caddis larva. Pupae are best imitated with a LaFontaine Deep pupa early in the hatch and a LaFontaine Emerging pupa when adults are in the air. Egg-laying females can be imitated with a Henryville

Special or Tan Elk Hair Caddis, but you will often have to pull the fly under the surface to get results. A Spent Caddis pattern in tan might be a better idea.

Small Gray Caddis (Glossosoma, Psilotreta, and other species). These caddisflies form tiny stone cases in fast water. The larvae eventually outgrow their cases and have to leave them to form new ones. Many get washed away and are eaten by trout in the process. Pupae hatch throughout the day, usually not in great numbers. However, females return to the water in the

When Small Gray Caddis larvae outgrow their cases, they become easy prey for trout.

The Small Gray Caddis can be difficult to see on the water.

This caddis imitation is supposed to look like the larva sticking out of its case.

evening in concentrated numbers and can really bring trout to the surface. One of the most frustrating aspects of this insect is that when the adults are laying eggs, the tiny dark insects are almost impossible to see. If you see rises on a May or June evening but can't see any insects, this one may be the culprit. Larvae are imitated with a Buckskin or Cased Caddis larva. Pupae are imitated by a small gray or green LaFontaine Deep pupa before the hatch and a dark green X-Caddis for emerging adults. For egg-laying females, use a small dark Spent Caddis or Black Soft Hackle.

Gary LaFontaine's Deep pupa is one of the best caddis pupa imitations ever developed.

The X-Caddis imitates both emerging and adult caddisflies.

SUGGESTED FLY PATTERNS

Pattern	Nymphs and Wets Sizes	Region and Season
Hare's Ear nymph	12, 14, 16, 18	All regions, April–October.
Bead-Head Caddis	14, 16	All regions, April–October. Pupa in green, tan, and gray.

Nymphs and Wets (cont.)

Pattern	Sizes	Region and Season
LaFontaine Deep	14, 16	All regions, April–October. Pupa in olive and tan.
Green and Tan Caddis larva	12, 14, 16	All regions, April–October.
Hare's Ear Wet Fly	12, 14, 16	All regions, April–October.
Partridge and Orange Soft Hackle	12, 14, 16	All regions, April–October.

Dries

Pattern	Sizes	Region and Season
X-Caddis in tan, green, and black	12, 14, 16, 18	All regions, April–October.
Elk Hair Caddis in tan, olive, and black	12, 14, 16, 18	All regions, May–October.
Henryville Special	12, 14, 16	All regions, May–June.
Spent Caddis (many different types) in tan, green, gray, and black	12, 14, 16, 18	All regions, May–October.

FISHING STRATEGIES

No caddis larvae can swim and none drift far from the bottom, so all caddis larva imitations should be fished dead drift and as close to the bottom as possible. This typically means putting weight on the leader, a strike indicator, and either a straight upstream presentation or an up-stream-and-across presentation with a high rod tip and as much line as possible off the water. Larvae are best fished in the morning as the nocturnal drift is finishing, but larvae can be a good fly pattern to use any time you see no other activity.

Once you see a few adult caddisflies in the air or you suspect a caddis hatch, switch to either a Deep pupa or a Bead-Head pattern. Fish these the same way—dead drift close to the bottom—but introduce a twitch once in a while or actually make the fly rise to the surface at the end of the swing by lifting your rod tip. You can also try casting across and downstream to get the fly to swing across the current, but remove the strike indicator and any weight on the leader before you do this to let the fly swing properly. Although making the fly rise to the surface can be deadly at times and it makes sense, based on the behavior of caddis pupae, I am far more successful fishing caddis pupae dead drift.

Once you see trout feeding on the surface regularly, switch to an emerging caddis pattern, such as an X-Caddis or LaFontaine Emerging pupa. Or take a standard caddis dry fly, such as the Elk Hair Caddis, and pull it under the surface. Unless you see pupae swimming across the surface, it's best to fish these flies dead drift, as you would a standard dry fly. You can also try an Elk Hair Caddis with a pupa tied to the bend of the hook on a short piece of tippet, using the Elk Hair Caddis as an indicator.

If you are certain trout are feeding on adult caddisflies on the surface and not the emergers, you can fish a caddis dry fly dead drift, just as you would a mayfly. Because trout often follow the pupa to the surface and then take the adult as it emerges, it's important to hit the rise form as quickly as possible with your imitation. Only when trout are sipping adult caddisflies without splashy rises should you worry about rise rhythms and timing. If caddis are skittering across the surface, you can impart some movement to your fly. One way is to throw an upstream curve cast or cast downstream to a rise with some slack, and then move the fly upstream an inch by raising your rod tip followed by a dead drift. The fly must always move upstream—if it moves down, trout will refuse it every time. Another method, sometimes used when few flies are on the water, is to grease your fly and entire leader with paste fly flotant, cast across and downstream, and skitter the fly across the surface by raising your rod tip while twitching it. This method works particularly well in the smooth water at the tails of pools, where a conventional dry-fly presentation is difficult.

If you see egg-laying females returning to the water, try to figure out what they are doing. If you see them spent on the surface, fish a low-floating dry fly absolutely dead drift. If the females are skittering across the surface and dive bombing the water with eggs, try a higher-floating dry with an occasional twitch. And don't forget that even though you see adult caddis on the water or in the air, trout may be eating most of them underwater as they dive just below the surface to lay eggs. Try a wet fly swung in the current in an across-stream presentation or dead drift. After dark, switch to a wet fly about the same size and shade as the naturals and fish it across and downstream on a slow swing with plenty of mends. This technique works particularly well in slow pools and can often get you a few extra trout after the hatch is over.

7

Stoneflies

STONEFLIES ARE INSECTS OF FAST, OXY-
genated water. They are seldom a dominant food source
for trout, except for brief periods when certain large species are active. They are far more important in the western part of the country than in the East and Midwest.

LIFE HISTORY

Stoneflies undergo incomplete metamorphosis because they do not have a pupal form. The aquatic larvae
live underwater for one to four years; the larger insects
are more likely to spend multiple years as a larva. Stonefly nymphs live only in tumbling, highly oxygenated water. They are more common in headwater mountain
streams and whitewater stretches of bigger rivers. They
are seldom found in lakes, spring creeks, or slow pools.
Nymphs live most of their lives secluded under flat rocks,
avoiding exposure to light and currents.

A few days prior to hatching, nymphs migrate into shallow water. At this point, they are exposed and often get swept into the current. Because they cannot swim at all, they may drift for many yards before reclaiming a spot on the bottom. Most species of stoneflies crawl onto rocks or logs along the shore, where they split their skin and hatch into adults, which look exactly like the nymphs except for the addition of wings. Some crawl only a few inches onto shore, while others may crawl twenty feet up into the brush or onto a tree trunk before they hatch.

Adult stoneflies live up to four weeks in streamside vegetation. Some take only liquids; others feed on plants or lichen. Males and females mate on the ground or under broad leaves. Females return to the water to lay eggs; in most species they dip their abdomens on the surface to drop the eggs, but in a few the females skitter across the surface as they deposit eggs. Stoneflies do not necessarily fall spent to the water after laying their eggs.

IMPORTANT STAGES

There are only two short periods in a stonefly's life cycle when it is anything more than occasional trout food: 1) When nymphs are migrating into the shallows prior to hatching, and 2) when females return to the water to lay eggs.

In areas where stonefly nymphs occur, some will always be around, because these larvae live more than a year underwater and thus contribute to the overall food supply of trout. People or cattle wading in a river dislodge stonefly nymphs or they get swept away during floods. They also become part of the nocturnal drift and so get eaten by trout at night and early in the morning. But the nymphs are most important as trout food when migrating en masse prior to a hatch. Trout may even feed selectively on the nymphs at such times. You will know what kind of nymph to use by looking on streamside rocks, logs, or tree trunks that grow near the bank. The shed skins of stonefly larvae are perfect facsimiles of the nymphs in shape, size, and even color.

Stonefly nymphs are only found in fast currents, so the ideal water to fish one of these nymphs has a steep slope, lots of white water, and large rocks. Generally, the larger the rocks, the bigger and flatter the stonefly nymphs. You will also see adult stoneflies in the brush along the banks. Because they also resemble the nymphs, fish a nymph closest to the adult in size and color.

Unless you see the adults tumbling into the water and you see trout rising along the banks, don't bother imitating the adults. The air will be full of females during egg-laying flights. They are clumsy fliers and fall to the water both in the process of laying their eggs and just in getting from one side of the river to the other. The adults can fall into any kind of water, and sometimes you will find trout feeding on them far from the tumbling water that hatched them.

Stonefly nymphs, and especially the adults, are far more important west of the Mississippi than in the East. In fact, in my thirty-five years of fly fishing in the East, I've rarely seen trout feed on adult stoneflies. It seems that trout ignore them unless there is no other food present. Because stoneflies can be the only aquatic insect of any consequence in high mountain brooks, you will see trout taking the adults there. I once saw the air and water swarming with big, juicy Golden Stoneflies on the Delaware River in midafternoon—as heavy a flight of stoneflies as I had ever seen in the Rockies. Yet the trout completely ignored them even though water conditions were perfect. The Delaware is a rich stream full of mayflies, caddisflies, midges, minnows, and crustaceans; there were apparently too many choice insects for the trout to bother with stoneflies.

Some stonefly species hatch in the middle of the winter, and you'll see the tiny dark brown ones running along snowbanks on trout streams all over the country. However, prime stonefly time is June and July.

SOME IMPORTANT SPECIES

Giant Stonefly nymphs can live several years before hatching and thus grow quite large.

Giant Stonefly or Salmonfly (Pteronarcys species). This is the most important stonefly to western fly fishermen even though it does not occur in all rivers. Although I have collected a few of these nymphs on rivers in the Catskills, I have never seen one actually hatch in the East. This giant insect, as big as a size 4 when mature, brings up huge trout in shallow water. With its heavily speckled wings and black-and-orange body, you will never mistake it for anything else. If you did not know this gentle and clumsy insect was a herbivore, you would probably run away if you saw one fly or crawl toward you! In big rivers, such as the Deschutes in Oregon, the

Giant Stoneflies only hatch for a few days in any one place, but they bring the largest trout in the river to the surface.

Madison, Big Hole, and Yellowstone in Montana, or the South and Henry's Forks of the Snake in Idaho, this hatch is the biggest event of the year. Fishing nymphs is a better bet in the long run, as trout eat them weeks before the hatch and sometimes prefer them to the adults during a hatch or mating flight. But if you ever see the big adults getting into the water and trout eating them, you will never be without some monstrous dry flies in your box again. After the adults hatch, they get blown into the water, fall off branches, and enter the water while laying eggs. Usually, the adults start to warm up and fly in late morning; they continue to feed the trout for the rest of the day. Unfortunately, this hatch lasts for only a few days at any given point on a river, so catching the dry fly fishing is a matter of luck, exquisite timing, or a flexible schedule. A call to fly shops in the area or a search of Web sites might help you locate the hatch, though. Late June through early July are the best times to catch this hatch on most rivers.

The Golden Stonefly nymph is eaten by trout throughout the country.

Golden Stonefly (Hesperoperla or Calineuria species). In the West, this stonefly follows the Giant Stonefly, or Salmonfly, by about a week but lasts longer, sometimes two or three weeks. In the East, it hatches during June. Its habits and habitats are similar, though this smaller insect is not quite as clumsy as the Giant Stonefly. The adults are not as likely to get into the water unless the females are laying eggs. The nymph is a speckled yellow-brown; the adult is slightly lighter in color. The nymphs are important to trout and fly fishers in all parts of the country and are usually far more important as trout food than the adults.

Golden Stonefly adults are eagerly taken by western trout but often ignored by their eastern counterparts.

Yellow Sally or Little Yellow Stonefly (Isoperla species). This pale yellow to chartreuse stonefly lives mainly in mountain streams all over the country. You will find trout feeding on these insects in headwater streams from North Carolina to Nova Scotia to Oregon. Adults hatch later in the year than Golden Stones and can be seen all summer on some streams. When adults are hatching, trout will stuff themselves on migrating nymphs. When the females return to lay eggs on warm summer evenings, the trout may then feed selectively on the spent females with delicate sipping rises. This is the only stonefly adult I have ever seen eastern trout feed upon in any quantity; trout in small headwater brooks often feed heavily on them.

The Yellow Sally nymph is smaller and more delicate than most stoneflies.

Yellow Sally adults are a favorite trout food in mountain streams.

SUGGESTED FLY PATTERNS

Pattern	Nymphs Sizes	Region and Season
Kaufmann's Black Stone	2, 4, 6, 8	West Coast and Rocky Mountains, May–July.
Golden Stone	6, 8, 10, 12	All regions, May–July.
Hare's Ear nymph	8, 10, 12, 14	All regions, May–July.
Little Yellow Stone	14, 16, 18	All regions, June–August.

Generic stonefly imitations that simulate many species.

Pattern	Dries Sizes	Region and Season
Orange Stimulator, Improved Sofa Pillow, Henry's Fork Salmonfly, others	2, 4, 6, 8	West only, June–July.
Yellow Stimulator	6, 8, 10, 12, 14, 16, 18	All regions, June–August.

Randall Kaufmann's Stimulator is one of the best adult
stonefly imitations.

FISHING STRATEGIES

Nymphs should be fished in fast water close to the
bottom, completely dead drift. Heavily weighted flies,
weight on the leader, or even both should be used. Stoneflies cannot swim and don't rise to the surface as mayflies and caddisflies do, so any movement of your fly will
look unnatural. The best time to fish stonefly nymphs is
early in the morning in the East and from mid- to late

morning in the West. Still, trout may eat stonefly nymphs all day.

The bigger Salmonfly and Golden Stonefly dries can be fished either dead drift or with twitches—try both tactics. On the South Fork of the Snake in Idaho, legendary guide Joe Bressler showed me a radical method he uses to fish these big dries. He casts his fly to the bank, then twitches it away from the bank aggressively as you would a streamer. Next, he lets the fly drift without motion for a moment. The strikes are absolutely vicious. Imitations of the Little Yellow Stones are best fished without any motion and with a fly that sits fairly low in the water to imitate spent females.

8

Midges

LIFE HISTORY

MIDGES ARE A FAMILY OF TRUE FLIES IN the order Diptera. Midges are instantly identifiable because they have only one pair of wings. They are found in all waters, from stagnant lakes to rushing streams. They hatch all year, even in the dead of winter, so despite their tiny size they are always available to trout.

Midges undergo complete metamorphosis, with a larva, pupa, and adult form. Larvae live in mud and silt on the bottom of streams and lakes. In fact, you'll find them any place in a stream where debris collects. They are wormlike, with a small head and short feeble legs, and are generally red, green, or brown in color. Midge larvae are especially common in spring creeks and slow tailwater rivers where silty bottoms are the rule. The larvae form cocoons and pupate, emerging in about a week. The pupae rise slowly to the surface and thus are available to trout for a long period of time, especially in lakes and deep pools where they may have to rise slowly from the depths. The tiny pupae don't have much mass, so breaking the surface film is difficult for them, more so if the surface is calm or smooth. Most pupae are a dull brownish olive. Midges hatch all day long. During winter, this usually happens during the day; later in the season, most midges will hatch in the early morning and evening.

Adults hatch and take wing quickly unless the water is cold or it's raining. The adults mate on shore or on the surface of the water, often forming huge mating swarms consisting of thousands of insects hovering over a few feet of water. Fertilized females quickly enter the water to lay their eggs on vegetation, midstream rocks, or weed beds. The midge adults you see most often will have a brown-and-black ringed body and clear wings, but they can also be olive, gray, or cream. They range from a size 14, which is hardly what you would call a "midge," to a smaller size than you could ever imitate. Most stream-dwellers are size 18, 20, or 22.

IMPORTANT STAGES

As with many aquatic insects, the most important stages to trout are when pupae are drifting, trying to penetrate the surface film, and when females are returning to the water to lay eggs. Larvae are often hidden in the silt and recently hatched adults leave the water quickly.

In most trout streams, midges become extremely important as trout food under two circumstances: 1) When they are so abundant that trout can graze on them with little effort, and 2) during winter, when no other aquatic insects are active and available to trout.

There are many tailwater rivers in the western United States where midge larvae are so abundant that they literally carpet the bottom. Any disturbance, whether by wading or daily water fluctuations below a dam, puts hundreds of thousands of these tiny larvae into the drift.

Small but abundant, midge larvae can be found in copious numbers below dams.

In the South Platte in Colorado, the Bighorn in Montana, and the San Juan River of New Mexico, this situation can drive you crazy. You can't help but stir up midge larvae as you wade, and the trout have become conditioned to follow anglers all over the river like puppies, gulping the trail of free food you stir up behind you. Unfortunately, this sometimes leads to a despicable habit called shuffling, where a so-called angler stirs up the sediments on purpose and then lowers a fly just below his rod tip. Don't do it—this is definitely not a sporting thing to do. Even under normal conditions, there are always enough drifting midge larvae to keep trout active.

Many spring creeks host more midges than any other type of insects combined. I grew up fishing a spring creek

Midge pupae drift helplessly in the film and are easy targets for trout.

that had a moderate mayfly hatch in April and no stone-flies or caddisflies. Almost our entire repertoire on that little stream consisted of midge larvae, pupae, and adult patterns. My fly box looked like a box full of staples and pins.

Another abundance occurs when so many hatching midge pupae or adults returning to the water overshadow the presence of any other insect. In this case, trout will feed on the midges, even to the exclusion of bigger may-flies and caddisflies.

In rivers with smaller populations of midges, trout eat them from late fall to early spring but ignore them during mayfly and caddisfly hatches. Midges will almost always

Midge adults are particularly attractive to trout when they form clusters.

be found hatching in smooth, slow water. Because feeding trout need to hang suspended in the surface film, they typically feed on midges away from fast currents, in the most sheltered parts of a pool with enough current to bring the midges to them. During hatches and mating swarms, the diminutive midge adults can all be blown to one side of the river or even in one tiny pocket of a stream. I remember one windy April morning on Armstrong Spring Creek in Montana when it was only 25 degrees out and scores of trout were jammed into a tiny, bathtub-sized sheltered pocket in the creek. Every midge in the creek had been shoved there by the wind. Even though I had to return to my car almost screaming with pain every ten minutes because my hands were so cold, I had one of the best hours of dry fly fishing I had ever experienced.

SUGGESTED FLY PATTERNS

Pattern	Nymphs Sizes	Region and Season
Red Midge larva	14, 16, 18, 20, 22	West Coast and Rocky Mountains; eastern spring creeks. Ponds and lakes throughout trout range. All year long.
Green Midge larva	18, 20, 22	

Midge larvae are simple but effective flies.

Pattern	Nymphs (cont.) Sizes	Region and Season
Brassie	18, 20, 22, 24	All regions; most useful November–April, but year-round in spring creeks and tailwaters.
Disco Midge	18, 20, 22, 24	All regions; most useful November–April, but year-round in spring creeks and tailwaters.

Pattern	Dries Sizes	Region and Season
Griffith's Gnat	14, 16, 18, 20, 22, 24	All regions; most useful November–April, but year-round in spring creeks and tailwaters.
Palomino Midge	18, 20, 22	All regions; most useful November–April, but year-round in spring creeks and tailwaters.

Midge pupae, fished in the film, are deadly on sipping trout.

The Griffith's Gnat is a great imitation of a cluster of midges.

FISHING STRATEGIES

Midge larvae should be fished on light tippets with weight on the leader and a strike indicator. Most serious midge fishermen use two flies—a pupa imitation for the top fly and a larva tied to the eye of the upper fly with a six-inch piece of 6X tippet. Trout can often be seen swaying in the current, grazing on the abundant larvae. If the trout are in a spring creek or tailwater and are only moving a few inches as they feed, you can assume they are taking midge larvae or pupae. Also, if you know you are fishing a river with abundant midge populations but no fish are rising, use the same rig and blind-fish in places where the riffles flatten out in the middle of a pool. Even though midge larvae and pupae are found in silty areas, they can't swim and will drift through riffles. Strikes here are subtle and a strike indicator is almost a necessity.

If you see trout making soft, almost imperceptible rises and no spent mayflies or caddisflies are on the water, they are probably taking midge pupae, especially if it's winter or early spring. Resist the temptation to put on a dry. Instead, grease your leader right up to the fly and fish an unweighted midge pupa pattern, such as a Disco Midge or any other tiny brownish nymph without legs or tails. You will probably see the rise even though the trout takes your fly underneath the surface, or you will see your leader twitch in the smooth currents. If you must use a strike indicator when you think trout are eating midge pupae, make sure it's a small one and keep it well away from the fly, as trout are easily spooked when hanging so close to the surface. You might also try tying your midge pupa onto a larger dry fly, such as a Griffith's Gnat. The dry fly acts as a subtle indicator, and trout might eat it because it looks like a cluster of midges.

Trout, particularly small trout, will sometimes take adult midges skittering across the surface. You will usually do better with a pupa, but if you must fish a dry, grease

your leader and twitch a small hackled fly across the surface. This generally works better in lakes than in moving
water.

When adults return to the water in swarms, trout
will often key into groups that clump together. The famous Griffith's Gnat was designed specifically for this
purpose. Midge swarms don't clump every evening, but
when they do, dry fly fishing can be spectacular—to a
trout, a clump of two or three midges is as nice a
mouthful of food as a small mayfly. I have been lucky
enough to witness this several times on the Bighorn
River in Montana, when it seemed as if every trout in
the river was eating midges. One evening, I noticed the
trout passing up single and double midges—they were
only eating clumps of three or more! I was dumb-
founded. All of my midge patterns were too small and I
finally got the fish to eat a small black ant. Needless to
say, I never visit the Bighorn without plenty of size 14
and 16 Griffith's Gnats.

If trout are eating single midge adults or spent females,
try any small dry fly of the appropriate size and color and
fish it dead drift, just as you would any small mayfly pattern.

9

Other Aquatic Insects

NINETY PERCENT OF THE HATCHES YOU see on trout streams will consist of mayflies, caddisflies, stoneflies, or midges. However, other aquatic insects are regionally important in some rivers and in lakes. Following are the most common ones.

CRANEFLIES

Craneflies, like midges, are another family of true two-winged flies of the Diptera order. These big daddy longlegs you see on your screens at night hatch from wormlike larvae that live in mud along the banks of rivers and lakes. I had always thought the larvae were poor swimmers that got washed into the water and tumbled along like worms. But my friend Jim Cannon, owner of

Cranefly larvae are grubs.

The Blue Quill fly shop in Evergreen, Colorado, set me straight. He fished cranefly larvae on many Colorado rivers, especially the South Platte, and has observed these larvae swimming actively with an undulating motion. And they move quickly!

If you don't know whether craneflies occur in the rivers you fish, dig through the mud along the banks of a slow pool. If you find one- to two-inch maggotlike larvae without any other obvious features, you probably have craneflies in your river. Most of them are shades of orange, tan, brown, gray, or olive. High water washes the larvae out of their mud homes, so if the water rises, either dead drift a big drab nymph about 1½ inches long on the

Cranefly adults often buzz over the water in the early morning.

bottom or a slim leech pattern stripped like a streamer. These larvae stretch up to four inches long while swimming, so don't be afraid to go as big as a size 6.

Adult craneflies buzz along the surface to lay eggs. If you see big, fuzzy, mosquito-like forms brushing the water and trout are rising, try a size 12 Cream Variant or Brown Spider. You don't often see trout eating adult craneflies, but when you do it is usually early in the morning when no other flying insects are present.

WATER BOATMEN

These are aquatic bugs, family Corixidae. True bugs (order Hemiptera) can be distinguished from beetles by looking at their mouthparts. Bugs have piercing beaks, whereas beetles (order Coleoptera) have chewing mouthparts with jaws that are parallel to each other. Water bugs are active predators, and water boatmen swim through the water with sculling motions looking for prey or feeding on detritus. They are uncommon in rivers but abundant in most lakes. They undergo an incomplete metamorphosis and hatch from eggs into tiny adults. Water boatmen are active throughout spring and summer, and most of them overwinter as eggs.

Marty Cecil of Elk Trout Lodge, near Kremmling, Colorado, says these insects are not widely important as trout food. They do, however, provide fun fishing because they leave the water like missiles when they fly around and disperse. They also return to the water with big splats, attracting the attention of feeding trout. This happens at midday in August and September—the hotter and brighter the day, the better—and provides exciting fishing at a time when mayfly or damselfly hatches are sparse. A fly plopped into the water can often draw three or four fish at once, and strikes are explosive. If your fly is not taken immediately, retrieve it with short, abrupt strips.

Water boatmen create action during hot summer days when nothing else is active.

If you visited a fly shop in England, where still water fishing is far more popular and sophisticated than in North America, you might find a half-dozen imitations of corixa bugs, which are relatives of our water boatmen. In this country, you might find some flies tied by a local tier, but you would probably have to tie your own or make do with a standard nymph that looks something like a water boatman. A Bead-Head Caddis or a Flash-back Scud imitation in size 12 will work when water boatmen are active.

Trout also eat other aquatic bugs, such as backswim-mers and giant water bugs. However, it's not worth trying to identify or imitate these bugs, as they are occasional food and can be imitated by flies designed for other insects. One insect you do not want to imitate is the ubiquitous water strider, found on moving and still water throughout the world. Adult trout don't eat them. They apparently taste bad and are as hard as rocks. I once watched a seven-inch brown trout chase water striders for more than ten minutes; when the trout finally captured one, it spit the bug out instantly.

DOBSONFLIES, FISHFLIES, AND ALDERFLIES

Dobsonflies, fishflies, and alderflies are members of the order Megaloptera. As larvae, they range around the bottoms of rivers and lakes, preying on insects and small fish with their large, sharp mandibles. They are most often found in the lower, warmer stretches of trout streams, and the big dobsonflies, also known as hellgrammites in the larval stage, are an important food for smallmouth bass.

Dobsonflies, also known as hellgrammites, are eaten by smallmouth bass and large trout.

All the larvae can be imitated by large dark nymphs meant as stonefly imitations or black Woolly Buggers. It's doubtful you'll ever find trout feeding selectively on any of these larvae. However, big trout found in the lower stretches of eastern rivers may actively seek them out, and specific hellgrammite imitations can be found in fly shops.

One adult, the alderfly, provides excellent dry fly fishing on certain rivers, such as the Housatonic in Connecticut and the Androscoggin in New Hampshire. Both are large rivers with relatively high summer water temperatures. Known locally as the zebra caddis, this alderfly can be distinguished from a true caddisfly by its darkly striped wing and head, which is more beetle-like than the head of a caddisfly. Alderflies hatch along the

Alderflies hatch in profuse quantities but are not as common as other aquatic insects.

banks and on bridge abutments in June and July. They are clumsy fliers and are blown into the water by the slightest breeze. Since they hatch in great numbers, trout look for them and can get quite selective. A King's River Caddis in size 12 or any other caddis imitation tied with turkey wings will work when alderflies are on the water. The fly can be fished dead drift or skittered across the surface.

As far as I can tell, alderflies are not common in any midwestern or western rivers.

Dragonfly nymphs aren't as active as damselfly larvae, but they are still eaten by trout in lakes and ponds.

DAMSELFLIES AND DRAGONFLIES

No one needs a lesson on how to identify these insects, which belong to the Odonata order. Damselfly larvae are slender, quick swimming insects. Dragonfly larvae are fatter and wider and swim by jet propulsion as they shoot water out of their rectal chambers. Adults hatch by crawling onto emergent vegetation. They spend a month or so eating mosquitoes and midges before mating and laying eggs. They overwinter as eggs or larvae buried in the mud, and some species live for up to four years in the larval stage. The nymphs become active in early spring as the water warms and then hibernate in the fall, so they are available to trout throughout the spring and summer months.

Damselflies are also more important to trout fishermen, as they are more active and abundant in the larval stage than dragonflies. Damselflies are also weaker fliers than dragonflies—some even crawl back into the water to lay eggs on vegetation in the middle of a lake—so trout are more likely to eat damselfly adults than dragonfly adults. Damselflies can be found in slow, weedy streams but are far more common and important in the shallows of lakes and ponds. The nymphs migrate into the shallows to hatch from late May through July, so many of them are

Damselfly nymphs are among the most important trout foods in still waters.

seen and eaten daily by trout. If you take a fly-fishing trip to a lake without some imitation of damselfly nymphs, you are starting with a disadvantage. These insects can be the primary food in still waters and trout are always on the lookout for them.

Damselfly nymphs should incorporate marabou or some other soft material because of the way these insects wiggle when they swim. You'll sometimes see stiff, realistic flies, but these look better than they work. In a pinch, an Olive Woolly Bugger in size 10 or 12 is a fine imitation of a damselfly nymph. The best way to fish these

Damselfly adults crawl into the water to lay eggs, and trout can feed selectively on them.

nymphs is to sight-fish in the shallows at midmorning, when any trout cruising in the shallows will be feeding. Cast well ahead of a cruising trout and retrieve the fly with short strips as the trout gets within a few feet of your fly. If the water is too deep or the weather is cloudy, blind-fish a damselfly nymph in the shallows by casting over weed beds, and retrieve it with a steady movement.

Damselfly adults are occasionally blown into the water. During the rare times when trout eat them, you'll have trouble getting a strike without a specific imitation of one, because nothing in your fly box will be the right size, shape, or color. I have been caught without damselfly dries in my box on high Montana lakes, and as a result missed some exciting sport. The Parachute Damsel in size 12 should be all you need.

10

Terrestrial Insects

INSECTS THAT AREN'T BRED IN THE WATER but live along the shore may tumble or fly into the flow and be eagerly inhaled by trout. In small streams, without vast riffles where aquatic insects breed and with more shoreline per mile of water, terrestrial insects provide up to 80 percent of a trout's diet from May through September. However, only rarely do trout feed selectively on terrestrial insects, so a grasshopper or beetle imitation in a specific size and color is not as important as having a fly that looks similar to the beetles or grasshoppers that trout recognize. Imitating these insects can lengthen your dry fly fishing into hours when no aquatic insects are hatching. The more common and important terrestrial species are discussed on the following pages.

ANTS

Trout love ants and seem to go out of their way to eat them. One of the best tricks for taking a trout that is feeding selectively on mayflies, caddisflies, or midges is to toss a small ant imitation over the fish. Ants become active as soon as the air temperature exceeds 50 degrees Fahrenheit, and as the season progresses and vegetation

An ant imitation can be a valuable addition to your fly box.

extends over the water, they tumble off their perches more often. Ants work from midmorning through evening. They are a good bet when you see no trout rising or see only a few dimples along the banks in the middle of the day. Any place with water that is more than a foot deep with a slow to moderate current flowing up against a bank is good ant water, especially if you see some ants on the water or in the surface film. Fish directly upstream along the banks without imparting any motion to your dry fly.

I think you can get by anywhere in the country with two ant imitations—a size 14 black one to imitate carpenter ants and a size 18 tan one to imitate the smaller cinnamon ants. Try to find imitations with either a white parachute wing or a piece of orange yarn tied on top, as ant flies should ride low in the surface film and be nearly impossible to see.

Species of ants disperse into new territories from late spring through early fall. Certain individuals in a colony develop wings, and something about the surface of a stream or lake must attract them, because they fall into the water in great numbers. These flights usually last only a day or two, but when they do, trout feed with the abandon more typical of a heavy mayfly or caddisfly hatch. If you don't recognize the situation, fishing can be frustrating. I have seen most carpenter ant flights on clear, calm days in late afternoon in June. The tiny brown ants seem to take flight in late August on still, muggy days from 5 p.m. until dark. If you fished every day of the season, you might need a flying ant imitation on only one day, but it's worth devoting a few inches in your fly box to some size 16 Black Flying Ants and size 20 Tan Flying Ants.

BEETLES

Beetles, like ants, are active and abundant from late May until the first frost. Unlike ants, adult beetles are capable of flying all the time. They tend to be clumsier than ants, so trout probably see them fall into the water more often. Apart from years when an outbreak of Japanese beetles happens, I don't think trout feed selectively on beetles. If you can find a trout that is not feeding selectively on a hatch and is looking at the surface for food, and you can make a presentation without spooking the fish, you can probably catch the fish on a beetle.

I have my best luck fishing beetles in late afternoon in fast water that runs along the bank or under trees. I know beetles are active at this time of day, and by sticking to fast water, I can usually avoid spooking trout with my approach and presentation. This strategy works in small New England brooks, as well as on big western rivers; in fact, my best dry fly fishing on Montana's Madison River

Trout like to eat Japanese beetles when there is an out-break.

is usually at midday with beetles when you seldom see any rises. A small twitch may sometimes get a trout to notice your fly, but you will usually overdo it and make the fly look unnatural. It's probably best to stick to a dead drift imitation; try to attract the fish with a soft plop as your fly hits the water.

Beetles can be cast hard to attract a trout's attention, but make sure your presentation makes the fly—not the whole line and leader—slap the water. The best way to do this is to give a quick downward flip of your wrist when completing the forward cast. As with ant imitations, try to find beetle imitations that have a red spot painted on the back or a piece of white or orange yarn on top for visibility. Because nearly all beetles are iridescent black on the ventral side, which is the only side a trout sees, I think you can get by with a pattern that's either all black or has peacock herl for a body. Sizes 14 and 18 should handle all your beetle encounters.

GRASSHOPPERS AND CRICKETS

Grasshoppers provide some of the best dry fly fishing of the season in the West, so many fishermen plan their vacations around grasshopper time. Trout in the East also feed on grasshoppers, but eastern streams don't have the vast grasslands that can produce hordes of these agricultural nightmares. Grasshoppers hatch in the early summer as small nymphs and grow quickly as the weather warms. By mid-July they can be swarming all over fields at midday, and you don't need an insect net or entomology lesson to know when they start getting important to trout. Grasshoppers live well into October in many areas, surviving through the first early frosts and coming back during warm spells.

Grasshopper fishing is wonderful; it's easy, nontechnical, and exhilarating. You can slap your fly onto the water, twitch the fly, or even let it drag. The fishing only gets difficult in rivers where trout see a lot of artificials and refuse to move more than a few inches to take a

Fishing grasshopper imitations is one of summer's greatest pleasures.

fly. Sometimes they seem to look the fly over for several feet of drift—they may even touch the fly with their noses, as if to smell your imitation! Although grasshoppers most often fall into the water near the banks, and trout move into shallow water to eat them, the current can also pull them into the middle of the river, so a grasshopper imitation will work almost anywhere. Grasshopper fishing is best from late morning to early afternoon when the weather warms enough to get insects active, and then the wind picks up, blowing these clumsy fliers into the water. If you can be the first wader or drift boat to fish a bank in late morning, you can be assured of great fishing.

Grasshoppers make quite a fuss when they fall into the water; they often try to swim to shore. Sometimes they get fatigued from swimming and will drift without any movement at all. I think you are better off fishing a grasshopper imitation dead drift unless trout totally ignore it, because trying to impart a realistic motion to a fly can often ruin a presentation, as the tendency is to overdo it. If you find that trout won't take your hopper without movement, make your twitches short and subtle—just enough to let the fish know your fly is "alive."

Your fly should be close to the naturals in size, as most of the hoppers might be size 12 this week but might have grown to a size 8 when you come back two weeks later. Most hoppers have tan, yellow, or green bodies, and it's probably safe, but not critical, to match the body color of the naturals. You can comfort yourself, though, with the fact that there are probably several species and sizes falling into the water on any given day, and the trout won't choose one over the other. There are scores of great hopper imitations available. My favorites are the Letort Hopper and Parachute Hopper in sizes 6 though 12, because although hopper flies are big, they ride low in the water, and these two patterns are easier to see.

Crickets are nowhere near as abundant or important as hoppers along trout streams, but trout eat them when they tumble into the water. The fishing techniques are the same. Crickets are more likely to be found in forested areas than hoppers, so they can provide good fishing in headwater brooks. All you should ever need is a size 12 Letort Cricket.

CICADAS

Cicadas are also called hot bugs because they sing in hot weather, and seventeen-year locusts because some

Cicadas are eaten by trout on desert rivers of the southern Rockies.

species have seventeen-year cycles of abundance. You are unlikely to see trout taking them anywhere other than high desert rivers in the West, specifically the Green River in Utah and the Dolores in Colorado. These insects are found near groves of juniper trees. They either tumble or are blown into the water, like grasshoppers. The opportunity to fish for trout with a size 4 dry fly is rare anywhere in the world, so fishing imitations of these bugs is quite popular. There are specific imitations of cicadas, but a large Chernobyl Ant, Tarantula, or even a fat hopper imitation will catch trout when they are looking for cicadas.

SPRUCE BUDWORMS

Periodic outbreaks of these moths in conifer forests can offer the dry fly fisherman extra sport during midday in high summer when there are few other insects on the water. Look for the moths in shady spots in a river under trees and in places where hillsides are covered with spruces. The larvae cause extensive damage to spruce trees when they are abundant. If you see white moths flying close to the water, they are probably spruce budworms, which are primarily terrestrial but fly into the water regularly.

These moths can be found on trout streams in mountainous regions throughout the country. They can also be abundant on high mountain lakes in the Rockies. If you happen to see them, fish a size 10 or 12 Elk Hair Caddis in tan or white. Your fly can hit the water with a splat, because the moths make a pretty big disturbance when they hit the water.

LEAFHOPPERS

These little bugs are similar to beetles but smaller and generally green or yellow. They live in all kinds of vegetation and may literally carpet the water on windy days. These bugs are so abundant that they provided the inspiration for the first modern terrestrial fly, Vince Marinaro's Jassid. It's also a fly near and dear to my heart, because I caught my first trout on a Jassid. Trout sipping along the banks in the middle of the day will often be taking leafhoppers. You can probably get by with a small beetle when trying to imitate leafhoppers, but since the naturals are so much smaller and lighter in color than most beetles, I like to carry a few Jassids or Leafhoppers in my box for summer fishing. A pale green one in size 20 or 22 should be sufficient.

INCHWORMS

These small green caterpillars hang over trout streams on fragile silk threads in late spring, and trout eat lots of them. I doubt if trout feed selectively on inchworms, but they do recognize them as food. An inchworm falling into the water is easier to imitate than a caddisfly emerging from the bottom of a river. Inchworm imitations are simple and usually constructed with chartreuse deer hair or foam. Fish them under trees in a size 14 during the day, and don't worry if your fly sinks. Inchworms do, too, and trout will eat them just as eagerly under the surface.

Inchworms fall into streams, and trout wait for them.

I suspect trout may eat other caterpillars as well, particularly when there are outbreaks of insects such as the gypsy moth. However, over the years I have tried my own imitations of locally abundant caterpillars with mediocre results, and I suspect many of the naturals don't taste good to trout. Thus, I don't think you have to worry about carrying a selection of caterpillars in your fly box.

11

Crustaceans

CRUSTACEANS DON'T HATCH AND LEAVE the water as aquatic insects do, so they provide food for trout all year in the same stage. Imitating them is very simple. You will find crustaceans most often in alkaline or hard-water streams and less often in northern, acidic, tea-colored rivers. Crayfish are more common in rivers with flat rocks where they can hide; scuds and sowbugs will be more abundant in weedy waters. Simply turning over a few rocks in the shallows or looking for tracks and crayfish claws left by raccoons along the bank will alert you to the presence of crayfish. A handful of aquatic weeds can host scores of scuds and sowbugs if they are present. All crustaceans are high-energy foods, and trout go out of their way to eat them.

SCUDS AND SOWBUGS

Both of these crustaceans can be found in weedy lakes, spring creeks, and tailwaters. Scuds are compressed laterally, or from side to side. They swim actively, with a deliberate rolling motion. They are important trout foods in lakes and rivers. Sowbugs are also flat but compressed dorsally, or from top to bottom. They crawl among the weeds and don't swim. They are more important as trout food in streams than lakes because they get knocked off their weedy perches in streams and drift in the current. In

Scuds are only found in rich alkaline streams.

lakes they stay near the bottom, so trout don't see them often.

These invertebrates are important trout food where they occur, because trout can feed on them all winter long if the water does not get too cold. A fish that feeds all winter can not only be caught on a fly at that time but also is typically bigger, because it has a longer growing season.

Both scuds and sowbugs are more active when light levels are low. In fact, the best time to fish a scud imitation is early in the morning when the naturals are active and there is not much insect activity. A seldom-practiced but productive and fun way to fish with a nymph is to fish at first light over shallow weed beds in spring creeks or lakes. Trout can be seen cruising or hovering in place, sometimes even shaking mouthfuls of weeds to dislodge sowbugs and scuds. But scuds can be fished all day, during any season, in any kind of weather. In lakes, a slow, steady retrieve after letting the fly or sinking line get close to the bottom works best. In streams, a dead drift is far more effective, because although scuds can swim, they're often quite passive when they tumble off their weedy perches and into the current.

Scuds swim with their bodies held straight but are crescent-shaped at rest. Imitations used in still waters or slow streams should not look curved, but because most

The Flashback Scud is one of the most productive imitations.

scuds in faster water are taken while drifting inert, a curved imitation will work better in swift streams. Most scuds are gray, tan, or olive, and an imitation that combines all of these colors seems to be sufficient. The best imitation around is probably the Flashback Scud in sizes 12 through 18. Fish the bigger sizes in fast riffles and the smaller ones in slow pools. The traditional Beaver or Otter nymphs are better imitations in lakes and ponds. In streams where sowbugs are important, a Gray Sowbug in sizes 12 through 16 will be needed.

Scuds only turn pinkish orange when they are dead. Yet on some rivers, notably the Bighorn in Montana, an orange scud usually works better than an olive or gray one. I am not sure whether trout see many dead scuds

Sowbugs are not usually as abundant as scuds but are still an important crustacean in alkaline streams.

and prefer them or whether the orange fly is just more visible.

Both scuds and sowbugs occur in the same habitat, but scuds are usually more abundant. Even if you see trout feeding in the shallows over weed beds, there's no way to tell if they are feeding on scuds or sowbugs or if they are feeding selectively on either one. If you fish weed-filled waters, I would suggest that you start with a scud about the size of the ones you see after examining a clump of weeds. If your first fly choice doesn't work, try a smaller scud, as trout in heavily fished waters seem to be less suspicious of smaller imitations. Next try a scud in pink or orange. Finally, if no scud imitation works, tie on a sowbug.

MYSIS SHRIMP

Mysis shrimp were introduced into a few western rivers to provide food for landlocked kokanee salmon. The only trouble was that these little shrimp live on or near the bottom during the day and only rise to the surface at night, whereas kokanee salmon are daytime sight-feeders in the middle of the water column. An ironic benefit to this ill-advised introduction is that the shrimp get sucked out of lakes and into tailwaters, where trout lie in wait and dine on shrimp cocktails almost constantly. These fish

Mysis shrimp grow fat trout in western tailwaters. *Ross Purnell*

grow as fast as fish in a hatchery, and in places such as the Frying Pan and Taylor Rivers in Colorado, rainbow trout weighing more than ten pounds can be caught on tiny nymph patterns imitating Mysis shrimp.

Although these crustaceans are found in only a few tailwaters, imitations are important if you go there, because trout feed selectively on these shrimp, particularly in spring and fall. The shrimp have prominent black eyes. Their bodies are translucent when alive, creamy white when dead. They are a size 16 or 18, and trout eat them—dead or alive! Fish them dead drift on a light fluorocarbon tippet for stealth, because fishing pressure is heavy where trout eat them, and they see lots of imitations.

CRAYFISH

Wherever crayfish are found in lakes and rivers, you will find big trout, as well. Trout of all sizes eat these miniature freshwater lobsters whenever they can get them. Fish prefer them when they are shedding and their shells are soft but also track down and crush the hard-shelled ones with repeated attacks before swallowing them. The tiny young ones are especially favored, because they can be swallowed without difficulty, and their pincers are not as nasty.

Crayfish live in dens along mud banks, under rocks and logs, and in weed beds in rivers and lakes. They are inactive during the winter and start to prowl the depths when water temperatures hit about 50 degrees Fahrenheit. They have one brood of young per season, and the miniature varieties hatch and become active by early June. Crayfish are nocturnal, so trout eat them more often when they emerge from their hideouts in late evening or early morning.

Two kinds of flies are needed to imitate crayfish—a big Woolly Bugger or a specific crayfish imitation in size 4, 6, or 8 for the larger adults and a smaller nymph to imitate the young ones, which do not swim as well as adults and often drift helplessly in the current. The bigger streamer should be fished with quick strips and short pauses to imitate the motion of an adult scooting backwards, fleeing from a trout. You don't even have to worry about getting the fly too deep, as trout can see the big fly from far away. Also, crayfish sometimes dart toward the surface when trying to escape. Occasional long drifts can be interspersed with the strips, but if you slow down too much, you may give trout a reason to look over your fly and refuse it.

The smaller nymph, in a size 8 through 12, should be fished upstream, dead drift, without any action added to the presentation. The best time of year is June through early July when the young have just hatched. You can use a small crayfish imitation, but I have had better luck with a hard-bodied stonefly or a Hare's Ear nymph. A bonus is that large mayfly and stonefly nymphs are also active this time of year, so your nymph can imitate several types of food at once. These nymphs should be fished as close to the bottom as possible.

12

Other Trout Foods

LEECHES

LEECHES ARE ABUNDANT IN STILL WATERS, from tiny beaver ponds to big lakes. They are active twenty-four hours a day, twelve months a year, so they provide food for trout and fishing opportunities for us all year. Pick up a few rocks or turn over some logs along a shoreline to see if leeches are present. Or hang your foot over the side of a boat for a few minutes! Craig Matthews, owner of Blue Ribbon Flies in West Yellowstone, Montana, knows that trout go out of their way to capture leeches. To anyone who doubts the importance of leeches, Matthews has them observe while he throws a leech into the water in front of a cruising trout. The fish will always track down the leech and eat it, even if the fish has been feeding on mayflies.

Leeches are one of the most important trout foods in still waters.

Matthews says most people fish leeches too fast, too small, too thick, and too deep. When swimming, leeches stretch their bodies to several times their length at rest with a confident, undulating motion. Your fly should be fished in the same manner. Trout most often take leeches in shallow water near the surface, and you can sometimes see a big swirl as a trout grabs a leech.

Most leeches are a drab brown, olive, black, or tan. The exact color differs with water chemistry and species, but you can get by nearly everywhere with a black and a tan leech in size 8. In a pinch, even a Woolly Bugger will do just fine. However, one other possibility to consider is a fly shaped like a leech but with a highly visible color.

Leech flies should be thin and wiggly.

My fishing buddy Jim Lepage will not go into the Maine woods, or to any still water, without a box full of bright yellow leech patterns. There are no bright yellow leeches, but Jim is known for his ability to catch brook trout and landlocked salmon when no one else can.

AQUATIC WORMS

There are more than two hundred species of aquatic worms, all of which were related to our common terrestrial earthworm. Most of them have not been carefully studied, except perhaps the Tubifex worm, the carrier of whirling disease. Most aquatic worms are benign, however, and some species are an important part of the food chain. Because the freshwater species live on detritus, these aquatic worms are more common in streams—tailwaters, in particular—with a rich biomass.

Aquatic worms become important during a rise of water, such as when a rainstorm or dam release tears them loose from weeds and sand. They are more import-

Aquatic worms are available to trout when washed loose by high water.

ant in spring, when high water is prevalent, but trout will eat them any time the water level rises. Jim Cannon, owner of The Blue Quill fly shop in Evergreen, Colorado, has seen trout on the South Platte so stuffed with worms that they're still hanging out of the trout's mouths when caught. Most aquatic worms eaten by trout are

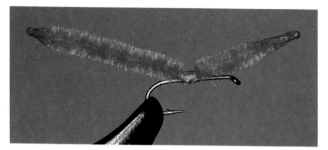

A simple worm fly made with a piece of chenille.

from ½ to 1½ inches long. They range in color from dark brown to tan to reddish orange. A tan imitation and a red one will probably cover any situation you encounter. The most popular patterns are the San Juan Worm and the Vernille San Juan Worm in sizes 8, 10, 12, and 14. These flies should be fished close to the bottom and dead drift, as aquatic worms do not swim.

BAITFISH

As trout get bigger, more of their diet is composed of other fish. But all sizes of trout eat other fish, and even a yearling trout will consume a just-hatched fry of its own species. It's mostly a matter of availability. Small fish are faster and more maneuverable than bigger trout and live in shallow water to avoid predation. But when water rises and pushes them into deeper water, or when water falls and forces them into deeper water as their habitat disappears, trout take advantage of the opportunity and prey on them with gusto. Trout also cruise into the shallows at night and early morning searching for baitfish.

I doubt that trout are often selective when feeding on baitfish in streams. However, it makes sense to use a fly that resembles prevailing baitfish species so it will be accepted by trout without hesitation. Streamers are taken most often, not only because they just look like a mouthful, but also because they resemble fleeing crayfish, leeches, cranefly larvae, and large swimming mayflies.

Other fish most often eaten by trout are their own young, as well as dace, darters, young suckers and whitefish, creek chubs, and sculpins. In lakes that have a large population of smelt or other baitfish, trout can become quite selective to size, shape, and color, so it's important to pay more attention to imitation in still waters.

SCULPINS

A reasonable approach to imitating baitfish is to look at them as two broad groups: 1) Slow bottom-dwellers that are flattened dorsally, such as darters and sculpins, and 2) the more typical streamlined fish of midwater. Sculpins are the most important baitfish in many streams, because they live out in the main current with trout, hid-

Sculpins are found in most trout streams and are easy for trout to capture.

den amongst stones on the bottom. When they move, they amble along close to the bottom where the current velocity is minimal. Trout see them every day, twelve months a year. Where trout over fourteen inches and sculpins live together, a great part of the trout's diet will be sculpins.

Fish sculpin imitations in fast water in places where there are lots of rocks on the bottom. The best presentation is to cast upstream and across, let the fly sink, and then strip about six inches at a time with a distinct pause in between. This imitates a sculpin darting from one rock sanctuary to another.

There are many sculpin patterns available, including the famous Muddler Minnow. My favorite is the Moto's Min-

Sculpin imitations feature the broad head and dull colors of the natural.

now, because its weighted head keeps it near the bottom, and its body, made of soft feathers, gives it a lifelike action. Fish this fly in small sizes—around size 10—in smaller streams, and use up to size 4 in bigger rivers.

MINNOWS

I include all other baitfish in this group, from dace to young trout. If you need to get technical, observe small fish in the shallows and choose a fly that is closest to them in size, shape, and color. Most baitfish have dark backs, light bellies, and either a horizontal stripe or vertical bars. If you carry a Black Nose Dace and an Olive Matuka in sizes 6 through 10, you will have most of them covered. I'd also throw in a brightly colored attractor, such as a Mickey Finn or Black Ghost Zonker, for visibility in dirty water.

Minnows and similar baitfish are better swimmers than sculpins and can really pour on the speed when pursued. Don't try to imitate the normal behavior of a baitfish. Instead, make it look like a bigger fish is pursuing the minnow, which evokes an instinctive reaction from trout. The best presentation is to cast across the river or across and downstream and experiment with retrieves. Unless the water is cold, I find the best retrieve is almost as fast as I can strip. You'll make your presentation more lifelike if you cast right to the bank or into the shallows, so it appears that another trout has pushed the minnow out of the protection of shallow water.

In still pools and in lakes, one type of streamer that is often overlooked is a crippled minnow. A baitfish that has been injured often floats to the top and struggles feebly. A floating streamer, such as a Muddler Minnow greased with fly flotant or a Crippled Smelt pattern, will often entice large trout to the surface. Fish these flies by casting upstream and across, twitching the fly as it drifts.

MICE AND OTHERS

Mice, frogs, snakes, salamanders, and small birds have all been found in trout stomachs. I am sure these are all targets of opportunity, and I don't suggest you worry about carrying a garter snake imitation. However, the importance of mice as food for large trout, particularly in the Rockies and in Alaska, has probably been understated over the years. Both Craig Matthews and Nick Lyons

A Hair Mouse can bring surprising rises in the middle of the day.

have told me some amazing stories of fishing mouse patterns for large brown trout.

Matthews says he fishes mouse patterns "Any time, any place, when all else fails. They always work on the Madison." And contrary to the popular belief that you need to fish a mouse pattern at night, he fishes them all day long, because mice and voles are active all day. Craig says you need a lot of movement, and the mouse fly should be fished close to the bank and stripped back toward the bank. You are trying to imitate a mouse that has fallen in by mistake and is trying to get back to shore, not one attempting to swim the English Channel. You can't fish one too close to shore. Craig has seen large trout eat mice right off the bank in the heat of a Montana summer afternoon.

Flies for this fishing don't need to be complicated. A simple Hair Mouse about 1½ long is all that's needed. You can be sure that the next time you see me on the Madison, I'll have a few in my box.

INDEX

A

Adams, 11, 69, 74
Adirondacks, 59
Alderflies, 126–128
Androscoggin River, 127
Ants, 17, 134–136
Aquatic worms, 157–159
Ausable River, 8

B

Bachman, Robert, 6–7
Baetis. *See* Blue-Winged Olives
Baitfish, 8, 159–160
Bead-Head Caddis, 75, 86, 92, 94, 126
Beaver nymph, 149
Beetles, 17, 124, 136–138, 143
Big Hole River, 102
Bighorn River, 113, 120, 149
Black Ghost Zonker, 163
Black Nose Dace, 163

Blue-Winged Olives, 57–59, 74

Brachycentrus (*See* Black Caddis), 82, 86–87

Brassie, 116

Buckskin nymph, 91

C

Caddisflies, 10, 12, 17–18, 20, 21–22, 24, 34–35, 38–39, 42, 45, 78–96

Calineuria. *See* Golden Stonefly

Callibaetis, 73, 75

Cannon, Jim, 121, 158

Catastrophic drift, 12–13

CDC, 72, 86

Cecil, Marty, 124

Chironomidae. *See* Midges

Cicadas, 141–142

Coffin Fly, 74

Craneflies, 121–123

Crayfish, 5, 8, 45, 153–154

Crickets, 138, 141

Crustaceans, 146–154

D

Damselflies, 129–132

Delaware River, 26, 100
Deschutes River, 101
Disco Midge, 116
Dobsonflies, 126–127
Dragonflies, 129–130
Drunella. *See* Western Green Drake

E

Elk Hair Caddis, 86, 95, 143
Elk Trout Lodge, 124
Ephemerella subvaria. *See* Hendrickson

F

Fishflies, 126
Flashback Scud, 126, 149
Flying Ants, 136
Frying Pan River, 152

G

Giant Stonefly, 101–103
Glossosoma. *See* Small Gray Caddis
Golden Stonefly, 100, 103–104, 106, 109
Grannom. *See* Black Caddis

Grasshoppers, 17, 138–141
Gray Fox, 72, 74
Green Drake, 29, 70–72, 74
Griffith's Gnat, 117, 118, 120

H

Hair Mouse, 164–165
Hare's Ear nymph, 59, 65, 73, 86, 92, 106, 154
Hare's Ear Wet Fly, 86, 93
Hellgrammites. *See* Dobsonflies.
Hendrickson, 42, 59–62, 73
Henry's Fork Salmonfly, 107
Henry's Forks of the Snake, 102
Henryville Special, 86–87
Hesperoperla. *See* Golden Stonefly
Housatonic River, 127
Hydropsyche, 82, 87–89

I

Improved Sofa Pillow, 107
Inchworms, 144–145
Isonychia, 57, 75
Isoperla. *See* Yellow Sally

J

Jassids, 143

K

Kaufmann's Black Stone, 106

L

LaFontaine Deep pupa, 86, 88, 91
LaFontaine Emerging pupa, 86, 95
LaFontaine, Gary, 82
Leafhoppers, 143
Leeches, 17, 155–157
Lepage, Jim, 157
Lepage's Bead-Head Mayfly, 73
Letort Cricket, 141
Letort Hopper, 140
Light Cahill, 72
Little Yellow Stonefly, 104–106, 109

M

Madison River, 78, 102, 136, 165
Maine, 59
March Brown, 23, 62–65, 72, 73

Matthews, Craig, 155
Matuka, 163
Mayflies, 9–10, 17–18, 20, 23, (24?), 26–29, 34, 38–39, 43, 45, 49, 51–77
McClennan, Jim, 69
Mice, 164–165
Mickey Finn, 163
Midge larvae, 17, 20
Midges, 17, 24, 28, 40–41, 48, 49, 110–120
Minnows, 17, 18, 45, 163–164
Mother's Day Caddis, 86
Muddler Minnow, 161
Mysis shrimp, 151–153

N

Nocturnal drift, 12

O

Olive Matuka, 163
Otter nymph, 149

P

Palomino Midge, 117

Pale Evening Dun, 65–67, 74

Pale Morning Dun, 65–67, 74

Parachute Damsel, 132

Parachute Hopper, 140

Partridge and Orange Soft Hackle, 93

Pheasant Tail nymph, 57, 67, 68, 73

Pit River, 78

Psilotreta. *See* Small Gray Caddis

Pteronarcys. *See* Giant Stonefly

R

Rusty Spinner, 59, 67, 72, 74

Ryacophila, *82*

S

San Juan River, 113

Scuds, 17, 45, 46, 146–151

Sculpins, 160–162

Shad Fly. *See* Black Caddis

Shuffling, 13, 113

Sipping, 7, 18, 25

Small Gray Caddis, 89, 90

South Fork of the Snake, 102, 109

South Platte River, 113, 122

Sowbugs, 17, 45, 46, 146–151
Spruce Budworms, 142, 143
Spruce Creek, 6
Stenonema fuscum. *See* Gray Fox
Stimulator, 107, 108
Stoneflies, 17, 24, 25, 28, 36–37, 40–41, 96–109,
    154

T

Taylor River, 152
Temperature, 7, 14–16
Tipulidae. *See* Craneflies
Tricorythodes. *See* Tricos
Tricos, 67–70

W

Water Boatmen, 124–126
Woolly Bugger, 127, 153, 156

X

X-Caddis, 91, 92, 94

Y

Yellow Sally, 104–106

Z

Zebra Caddis (Alderfly), 127
Zug Bug, 73

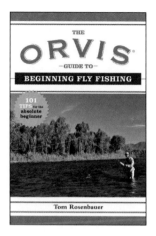

The Orvis Guide to Beginning Fly Fishing
101 Tips for the Absolute Beginner

by Tom Rosenbauer

This book, written with the support of America's oldest fishing tackle business, offers beginners a chance to learn the fundamentals of the great sport of fly fishing quickly and easily. *The Orvis Guide to Beginning Fly Fishing* can be the start of a lifetime journey of discovery that will increase your intimacy with the natural world and allow you to gain skill and finesse in your fly-fishing techniques. Proven teaching techniques and bright, helpful illustrations and photographs will enable new fly fishermen to:

* Select and assemble proper, balanced tackle
* Cast a line with authority and accuracy
* Chose the correct fly for any situation
* Tie the two most useful fishing knots
* Find fish in lakes, rivers, and salt water
* And much more

Here are fishing ethics, helpful safety advice, and basic angling terms— everything the new fly fisherman needs in a crisp, helpful, and finely illustrated primer of the highest rank.

$12.95 Paperback • ISBN 978-1-60239-323-3

ALSO AVAILABLE

The Orvis Guide to Beginning Fly Tying
101 Tips for the Absolute Beginner
by David Klausmeyer

This Orvis-endorsed guidebook—part of a continuing series that includes guidebooks on fly-fishing basics and saltwater fly fishing—will give you all the tools you need to begin making your own flies. Learn how to read a fly recipe, choose the correct tools (including vises, bobbins, threaders, dubbing needles, and hair stackers), select the right materials (everything from dry fly saddles, threads, beads, and Krystal Flash, to hooks, wires, cements, and paints), and pick the best flies to tie first. Before you know it, you'll be tying such flies as the Wooly Bugger, Clouser minnow, beadhead soft hackle nymphs, Adams dry fly, and Hare's Ear nymph. You'll also get solid advice on how to set up a well-organized fly-tying area, so you can enjoy this fascinating craft in ease and comfort.

Fly Tyer magazine editor David Klausmeyer shares his Five Golden Rules for tying better flies. Many books say they are for beginners but then quickly turn fly tying into a series of complicated finger calisthenics. *The Orvis Guide to Beginning Fly Tying* really is for the reader who has never made a fly. Catch fish with flies that you've tied on your own, and you'll get more enjoyment from the rich sport of fly fishing.

$12.95 Paperback • ISBN 978-1-61608-622-0

ALSO AVAILABLE

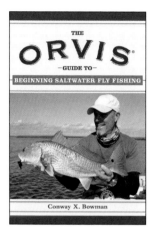

The Orvis Guide to Beginning Saltwater Fly Fishing
101 Tips for the Absolute Beginner
by Conway X. Bowman

Foreword by Kirk Deeter

Expert saltwater fly fisherman Conway Bowman offers advice and useful techniques for the beginner fisherman in *The Orvis Guide to Beginning Saltwater Fly Fishing*—ideal for the novice that wants to learn and perfect their skills. Written in conjunction with the prestigious Orvis Company, this all-encompassing guide is meant to teach and guide fishermen who wish to begin their adventure of saltwater fly fishing and don't know exactly how. Bowman answers questions ranging from what equipment is needed to how to identify saltwater fish to proven techniques to catch bigger and better fish.

This guide covers all the basics—from rods, reels, lines, and tippets to the actual art of identifying and catching fish to using the tides, moon, and weather in your favor—making it the key to fun and effective fishing. With hundreds of full-color photographs to accompany Bowman's nuggets of wisdom, *The Orvis Guide to Beginning Saltwater Fly Fishing* is the true companion for the outdoorsman who wants to catch top-notch fish.

$12.95 Paperback • ISBN 978-1-61608-090-7

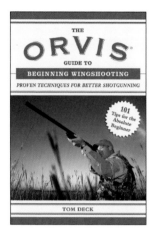

The Orvis Guide to Beginning Wingshooting
Proven Techniques for Better Shotgunning

by Tom Deck

The Orvis Guide to Beginning Wingshooting is required reading for anyone interested in picking up the sport or improving their shooting skills. Experienced shooter and teacher Tom Deck shares his tips, as well as insider tricks from the most successful wingshooters.

The Orvis Company began one of the very first shooting schools in America almost fifty years ago. Today, Orvis has schools, lodges, outfitters, and guides all dedicated to helping bird hunters discover and enjoy wingshooting. This book is a combination of the 101 best tips from many of the Orvis shooting instructors, outfitters, and guides.

It is packed full of expertise for the absolute beginner, but even the seasoned wingshooter will find some helpful tips to sharpen their skills. From the basics of gun safety, to learning how to correctly spread your duck decoys, *The Orvis Guide to Wingshooting* covers it all. Add this volume to your hunting shelf and you'll see a great improvement in your wingshooting technique.

$16.95 Paperback • ISBN 978-1-62087-619-0

ALSO AVAILABLE

The Orvis Streamside Guide to Approach and Presentation
Riffles, Runs, Pocket Water, and Much More
by Tom Rosenbauer

I know how to cast, I know my knots, and I can tell a dry from a wet fly. What next? This pocket guide shows the fly fisherman where to cast, why, and what kind of fly to use. It can be studied prior to a fishing trip or used in the water.

Streamers, nymphs, wets, and dry flies are detailed with diagrams and color photographs. The book is organized by water types, and once you identify what kind of water you are facing—riffles, runs, pocket water, or deep slow water—you can then decide what kind of fly to use, what leader is appropriate, and how to present the fly.

No more days of returning without a catch. With the extensive experience and knowledge of author Tom Rosenbauer, you can use his no-nonsense tips to identify appropriate fly-fishing wet and dry flies, adapt to current water conditions, and cast with confidence.

$12.95 Paperback • ISBN 978-1-62087-620-6